The Philadelphia Inquirer's

WALKING TOURS OF

HISTORIC
Philadelphia

FOURTH EDITION

EDWARD COLIMORE

D1536996

Camino Books, Inc.
Philadelphia

Manufactured in the United States of America

1 2 3 4 5   25 24 23 22 21

Library of Congress Cataloging-in-Publication Data

Names: Colimore, Edward, 1950– author.
Title: The Philadelphia Inquirer's walking tours of historic Philadelphia /
    Edward Colimore.
Other titles: Philadelphia inquirer (Philadelphia, Pa. : 1969)
Description: 4th edition. | Philadelphia : Camino Books, Inc, [2021] |
    Includes index.
Identifiers: LCCN 2021021784 (print) | LCCN 2021021785 (ebook) |
    ISBN 9781680980318 (trade paperback) | ISBN 9781680980509 (ebook)
Subjects: LCSH: Inuit (Pa.)—Tours. | Historic buildings—
    Pennsylvania—Philadelphia—Guidebooks. | Historic
    sites—Pennsylvania—Philadelphia—Guidebooks. | Walking—
    Pennsylvania—Philadelphia—Guidebooks. | Philadelphia (Pa.)—
    Buildings, structures, etc.—Guidebooks.
Classification: LCC F158.18 .C655 2020 (print) | LCC F158.18 (ebook) |
    DDC 917.48/1104—dc23
LC record available at https://lccn.loc.gov/2021021784
LC ebook record available at https://lccn.loc.gov/2021021785

Cover art: Robert Hochgertel
Cover design: Jerilyn DiCarlo
Interior layout: P. M. Gordon Associates, Inc.
Map design: Adriano Renzi copyright © Camino Books, Inc.

This book is available at a special discount on bulk purchases for
promotional, business, and educational use. For information write to:

Publisher
Camino Books, Inc.
P.O. Box 59026
Philadelphia, PA 19102

www.caminobooks.com

Dedication

To God, for inspiring William Penn to begin the
"Holy Experiment" he called Philadelphia.

To my wife Catia and son George,
for their company on many walks through the city.

And to my parents, James and Lucille,
for their love and support.

Contents

Acknowledgments

Any work such as this is a collective effort. I am grateful to the editors of the *Philadelphia Inquirer* for allowing me to walk through Philadelphia's rich history and share my experience with others—not only in this book but in countless newspaper stories during my thirty-three years as a staff writer and editor. This unique and rewarding project—now in its fourth edition—would not have been possible without their help and encouragement.

Special thanks must go to now-retired Special Projects Editor Lois Wark, whose encyclopedic knowledge of the city and devotion to the book were indispensable to its completion. From the very beginning, her enthusiasm, insight and ability as a wordsmith made this guide to historic Philadelphia a better, more user-friendly book.

I also wish to extend my sincere appreciation to Douglas Gordon for his keen-eyed edit of this latest edition and to former *Philadelphia Inquirer/Daily News* researcher Ed Voves, who was especially helpful in researching photographs and answering obscure historical questions.

Others deserve my particular recognition: my late mother, Lucille Colimore; my wife, Catia Colimore; and my son, George Colimore, for their love, support and patience over months while I immersed myself in the project. They sometimes joined me on walks through the city and allowed me to disappear for long hours with my computer, dusty books and notepads.

I might not have ever written this book apart from my father's influence. The late James Colimore was a World War II combat glider pilot who had an appreciation for history and a love for writing that showed in his newspaper column over many years in Baltimore. I owe much to him and the rest of my family—and dedicate this work to them.

Edward Colimore

Introduction

More than three centuries ago, William Penn set out to create a "Greene Country Towne," which would "never be burnt, and allways be wholsome." The new town would be a very different place from the congested, disease-plagued London of his time. Penn called his city a "Holy Experiment," a place of refuge for people longing to live in peace and worship freely. He envisioned thriving markets, handsome houses, orchards, gardens and fields—a veritable paradise. Philadelphia, he named it, the "City of Brotherly Love."

"And thou Philadelphia, the virgin settlement of this Province named before thou were born," wrote Penn in a prayer two years after the city's founding in 1682. "What love, What care, What service and What travail has there been to bring thee forth and preserve thee from such as would abuse and defile thee."

The love and travail are still very much present, as Philadelphians of the 21st century struggle to preserve the unique character of Penn's city. In the years between his time and ours, Philadelphia has become more like London in its crowding and griminess. Yet glimpses of the "greene country towne" remain in the proprietor's four lovely public squares and in the ribbons of greenery that roll back from the Schuylkill River in Fairmount Park, the nation's largest landscaped urban park.

Penn had set a tone for Philadelphia, imparting a certain tolerance and hospitality that drew people from many nations and creeds. In the 18th century, the city became the perfect backdrop for a heroic era of ideas that changed the world. This is the birthplace of the United States, where the Declaration of Independence and the Constitution were written and argued about. Some of the most treasured icons of American democracy are here—Independence Hall and the Liberty Bell, and the places where Benjamin Franklin and Betsy Ross lived and worked.

From the gathering of the first Continental Congress here in 1774 until President John Adams left 26 years later for the new capital in Washington, the greatest leaders of the emerging nation walked these streets, worshipped in these churches and lived out the most dramatic period of their lives.

This book walks you through Philadelphia's—and the nation's—early history. You'll see it unfold down quaint, cobblestoned alleys and busy, broad streets, in simple brick rowhouses and venerable mansions, in tiny courtyard gardens and magnificent parks. In these pages, you'll find the historical context of the buildings before you as well as guides to scores of out-of-the-way places. Along with the walks are tips on the modern city's amenities, including nearby restaurants, cafes, parking and public transportation.

Philadelphia is not one but several cities—and you can experience all of them if you know where to look. Tucked amid the glass-and-steel skyscrapers are not only the brick-and-mortar buildings of the colonial and Federal periods, but also blocks of homes from the Civil War era and the Age of Victoria.

What sets Philadelphia apart from many other cities is that it preserved, rather than bulldozed, much of its past. There are more historic structures here than in any other comparable American city, architecture critic Lewis Mumford once observed, primarily because so much history was made here. And there are abundant records and drawings of old Philadelphia buildings, making the restorer's job easier, because of the early presence of fire insurance companies, dating from the founding in 1752 of the Philadelphia Contributionship for Insurance of Houses from Loss by Fire. All of these things have combined to make Philadelphia an American time capsule, a unique museum of the nation's political, social, military and architectural history.

The neighborhoods that gave the city a comfortable human scale in times past are still here—along with the massive office towers. Society Hill, for example, stands today as a symbol of colonial Philadelphia—a part of the city that had fallen into slums by the turn of the 20th century but was restored in the late 1950s and '60s through an innovative plan of public-private development. Yet even on these quiet residential blocks of three- and four-story brick townhouses, the walker looks up to find modern apartment towers looming overhead. These collisions of past and present, mixed with discoveries along the way, make walking historic Philadelphia an experience of constant surprise and delight.

After a section of Useful Information, each tour begins with a brief overview and history of the area. The full walking tours, with an average of 20 stops, will occupy the better part of a day. Some tours—such as those taking in Fairmount Park, Germantown and Chestnut Hill—require driving as well as walking because of the distances involved.

Independence National Historical Park—site of Independence Hall, Congress Hall, Old City Hall, Carpenter's Hall and dozens of other historic places—has undergone major enhancements in recent years. The Independence Visitor Center (Sixth Street between Market and Arch Streets) opened in 2001 and has undergone a $15 million renovation wrapping up in 2019. The National Constitution Center (Sixth and Arch Streets), a national museum offering an interactive tour of American democracy, opened in 2003 and has also seen upgrades. A new Liberty Bell Center (Sixth and Chestnut Streets) opened in 2003, and underwent extensive landscape renovations in 2019. The building and grounds offer improved interpretation and surroundings for one of the nation's most revered icons. The changes have made better use of the sprawling 15-acre Independence Mall stretching from Race to Chestnut Streets

As you walk back in time, take a moment to reflect on the great men and women of the Revolution, going through their daily lives. Benjamin Franklin wrote about the pleasures of Philadelphia in a letter to a friend in 1786. He mentioned his family, friends, books and gardens. He wrote about balls, concerts, parties and card games. "I have indeed now and then a little compunction in reflecting that I spend time so idly; but another reflection comes to relieve me, whispering, 'You know that the soul is immortal; why then should you be such a niggard of a little time, when you have a whole eternity before you?'"

Indeed. Welcome to Philadelphia. Enjoy.

Edward Colimore

The Nation's Most Historic Square Mile

The Nation's Most Historic Square Mile

1. Welcome Park
2. Thomas Bond House
3. City Tavern
4. Merchants' Exchange (Philadelphia Exchange)
5. Independence Visitor Center
6. First Bank of the United States
7. Museum of the American Revolution
8. 18th-century-style garden
9. Bishop White House
10. 18th-century-style garden
11. Todd House
12. Carpenters' Hall
13. New Hall
14. Pemberton House
15. National Liberty Museum
16. Franklin Court
17. Benjamin Franklin Museum (underground)
18. Market Street Houses
19. Second Bank of the United States
20. Library Hall
21. Philosophical Hall
22. Independence Visitor Center
23. National Constitution Center
24. Old City Hall
25. Independence Hall
26. Independence Square
27. Congress Hall
28. Philadelphia History Museum
29. Declaration House (Graff House)
30. President's House
31. Liberty Bell Center

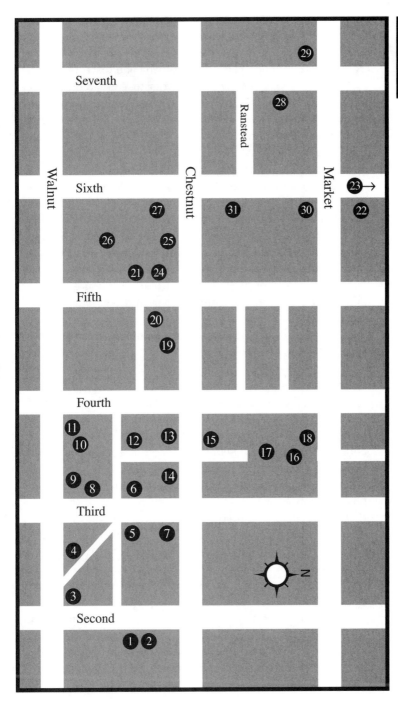

USEFUL INFORMATION

The Independence Park area has many fine restaurants and other eateries to fit any budget or taste. Among them: City Tavern, Second and Walnut Streets, which features a colonial-era menu and servers in 18th-century dress; Benton's Grill, Fourth and Arch Streets; and the Food Hall at the Bourse, Fifth Street near Chestnut, which was reinvented in 2018 with new food vendors and shops.

Several parking garages are nearby, including an underground facility beneath Independence Mall on Fifth Street between Market and Arch; a garage on Second Street between Chestnut and Walnut; and another on Seventh Street between Chestnut and Market. Signs direct visitors to other public parking lots as well.

Some suggestions: When you're ready for a break, stop in at the Bourse (on Fifth Street between Chestnut and Market Streets) for refreshments. This elegant building, with an atrium, wrought-iron stairway and Corinthian columns, was built in 1895 as a stock exchange.

Another way to get off your feet: Take a guided tour of the park, either by horse-drawn carriage or motorized Victorian trolley. Trolleys can be boarded daily at Fifth and Market Streets.

Horse-drawn carriages can be hired at Independence Hall and offer a pleasant, old-world diversion. The carriages, which line up at Fifth and Chestnut, offer various options, including a 20-minute, four-passenger ride for $50 and a half-hour, four-passenger ride for $60.

Your tours can be made easier with some knowledge of the public transportation system. SEPTA buses and the Market Street subway run through historic sections of the city, and you can hop on and hop off. SEPTA's Independence Pass is good for one day of unlimited transportation on all city transit vehicles, plus a one-way trip on the Airport Line.

Some basic geography: Center City is laid out on a grid, between two rivers—the Delaware on the east, the Schuylkill on the west. Starting at the Delaware River, Columbus Boulevard (Delaware Avenue) is the first north-south street, followed by Front, Second, Third, Fourth, Fifth, etc. Broad Street, the main north-south artery, is where 14th Street normally would be. Of the east-west streets, Market bisects Center City, intersecting Broad Street at the square where City Hall sits.

Buses run from Society Hill/South Street along Market Street and the Benjamin Franklin Parkway to the Philadelphia Museum of Art and the Philadelphia Zoo in Fairmount Park. Another bus route links Center City with University City. The R1 rail line connects Center City with Philadelphia International Airport. The Broad Street Line (subway) connects Center City with the sports complex in South Philadelphia. The PATCO High Speedline connects Center City with Camden and southern New Jersey.

The PHLASH, a colorful, purple vehicle, follows a downtown bus loop, stopping at the major tourist districts, including the Museum of the American Revolution, Benjamin Franklin Museum and Pennsylvania Convention Center. The shuttles make continuous runs from Logan Circle through Center City to the waterfront and South Street. There are no narrated tours. Cost is $2 for one trip or $5 for a day pass.

Introduction

No other collection of buildings is so rich with the history of the United States. No other conjures up so many images of its greatest leaders, or embraces so many memories of the debates that shaped the nation.

In elegant Carpenters' Hall, Americans spoke of liberty and sowed the seeds of revolution. At City Tavern, they argued over forms of government between glasses of Madeira and mugs of beer. And in the Assembly Room of stately Independence Hall, they declared their break from Britain with lofty, inspiring words: "We hold these truths to be self-evident: that all men are created equal. . . ."

The great men who walked the cobblestoned streets of Philadelphia—the "American Athens," some in the 18th century called it—have left their aura here. With only a little imagination, you can still encounter whiffs of them in 21st-century Philadelphia. Washington, Jefferson, Madison and Patrick Henry of Virginia. Hamilton, Jay and Gouverneur Morris of New York. Hancock and the Adamses, John and Samuel, of Massachusetts. And the incomparable Benjamin Franklin of Philadelphia—all living and working together here.

From the signing of the Declaration of Independence in 1776 to John Adams' departure for the new White House in Washington two dozen years later, these extraordinary men left an indelible mark on the city, transforming the area around Independence Hall into the most historic square mile in the nation.

Through the weeks of debate during that hot summer of 1776 leading up to the Declaration, passersby on Chestnut Street could hear them arguing through the windows thrown open to catch a breeze. A decade later, the wrangling was over the framing of a Constitution to govern the new nation. James Madison summed up the stakes during the Constitutional Convention in 1787: "The question on which the proposed Constitution must turn is the simple one whether the Union shall or shall not be continued."

When the great document finally was approved, an aged Ben Franklin offered up a speech to the convention, leaving it to his Pennsylvania colleague James Wilson to read it aloud. "It astonishes me, Sir," said Franklin, addressing himself to George Washington as convention president, "to find this system approaching so near to perfection as it does, and I think it will astonish our enemies, who are waiting with confidence to hear that our councils are confounded like those builders of Babel. I consent, Sir, to this Constitution because I expect no better and because I am not sure that it is not the best."

Over the years since that formative time, the face of Franklin's city has changed, to be sure. Some historic structures were neglected, others razed. But the most revered of them still stand, in a historic district of cobbled streets and colonial-style houses that is intimate in its feel and scale. They were tourist attractions in 1876, at the time of the nation's Centennial celebration in Philadelphia. In a souvenir book prepared for the Centennial Exhibition, author J.S. Ingram wrote that "Philadelphia possesses more relics of the past, more edifices around which hang a halo of history, than any other city in the Union."

The sites again were national tourist attractions in 1976, as vast numbers of people descended on the city for the Bicentennial celebrations, and in 1987, when they came for the Constitution's 200th anniversary. And the buildings and stories of the past continue to lure hundreds of thousands of visitors to Independence National Historical Park every year.

The sense of history—that halo described by Ingram—is strongest in the buildings at Independence Square. These are the structures that housed the Provincial Assembly, Council, Second Continental Congress, U.S. Senate, House of Representatives and Supreme Court. Here, the ties with Britain were severed. Here, independence was proclaimed on July 4, 1776. Here, the Liberty Bell was rung on the first reading of the formal declaration to the citizens of Philadelphia on July 8, 1776. Here, the United States of America came into being through the Articles of Confederation and the Constitution, which have inspired other countries and leaders around the world.

Little wonder that the area is considered the most historic square mile in the nation.

The Tour

Put on a pair of comfortable walking shoes, and we'll retrace the footsteps of the early patriots. We'll be starting on the eastern perimeter of the historic district, so you may want to park at the garage on Second Street between Chestnut and Walnut.

❶ Begin at **Welcome Park (1)** *(on Second Street and Sansom Street Alley between Chestnut and Walnut Streets)*, which helps tell the story of Philadelphia's earliest days. *Welcome* was the name of the ship that transported William Penn to America in October 1682.

The park was the site of the **Slate Roof House**, the home of William Penn and his wife, Hannah, during Penn's second visit to Philadelphia, from 1699 to 1701. The house was known for having the first slate roof in the American colonies. Here, Penn issued the Charter of Privileges in 1701, guaranteeing religious freedom and civil liberty to the residents of Pennsylvania. The charter served as the colony's constitutional framework and inspired legislators 50 years later to order a new bell for the State House to commemorate the document. It would become known as the Liberty Bell, one of the nation's most enduring symbols. Penn's sturdily built house did not endure, though. It was demolished in the 1860s.

In its place is a statue of Penn, a replica of Alexander Milne Calder's larger version atop City Hall. The statue stands in the middle of the park, overlooking a 60-foot-long map of old Philadelphia carved in stone and accompanied by historical notes on adjacent walls. Walk through the Philadelphia of 1682, as originally planned, following streets laid out in marble. Sit on one of the benches, notice the public squares planned by Penn and read the proprietor's words. "Of all the many places I have seen in the world," Penn wrote, "I remember not one better seated; so that it seems to me to have been appointed for a town." And describing the layout of the city, Penn wrote of his "Greene Country Towne," "The names of the Streets are mostly taken from the things that grow in the country, as Vine Street, Mulberry Street, Chestnut Street and the like."

2 Next to the park is the **Thomas Bond House (2)** (*129 South Second Street between Chestnut and Walnut Streets*), a restored brick house from about 1769 with 19th-century alterations, now a bed-and-breakfast inn. Bond was a skilled surgeon who joined Benjamin Franklin in founding the American Philosophical Society and Pennsylvania Hospital, the nation's first hospital. The house has 12 period-furnished guest rooms with private baths, telephones and TVs. A stay here includes a complimentary breakfast and evening wine and cheese. Prices range from $145 to $215. For reservations, call 800-845-2663.

3 Walking south, along brick sidewalks, you may catch the enticing aroma of food wafting from the **City Tavern (3)** (*Second and Walnut Streets*), a reconstruction of the imposing three-story hostelry that was built in 1773. Lunch service begins at 11:30 a.m., and dinner is served from 3 p.m. daily. (Open to the public.)

In colonial days, the tavern offered lodgings and well-appointed rooms for meetings, making it the focus of the social, business and political activities of the Philadelphia elite. From the informal debates here, the groundwork was laid for revolution and for the convening of a congress representing the colonies. The First Continental Congress held many unofficial gatherings at the popular tavern (500 attended one event, where men drank 33 toasts), and the Constitutional Convention held its closing banquet here as well. Among the notable guests was George Washington, who provided the recipe for a beer you can sample.

During the Constitutional Convention in 1787, Washington sat for a painting on July 6, then "dined at the City Tavern with some members of the Convention, and spent the evening at my lodgings," he wrote in his diary. Thomas Jefferson inspired some of the cuisine on

City Tavern

the tavern's menu. And John Adams once called the place the "most genteel tavern in America." Samuel and John Adams and Jefferson met here for "a feast of reason and flow of the soul."

The original tavern building was demolished in 1854—"immolated on the altar of improvement," as one newspaper said at the time. But its replacement is a faithful reconstruction. Across the street (*125 Walnut Street*) is a reproduction of the John Drinker house, built before 1760.

4 Leaving City Tavern, walk west on Walnut to Third Street. On the northeast corner of the intersection is the **Philadelphia Exchange**, also known as **Merchants' Exchange (4)** (*Third and Walnut Streets*), a magnificent, Greek Revival building considered one of the great creations of American architecture. (Not open to the public.)

Merchants' Exchange

For 50 years, this extraordinary structure served as the city's commercial hub, where stocks and commodities were traded and business was conducted. The oldest stock exchange in the nation, the building was designed by William Strickland, one of the foremost 19th-century architects, and erected between 1832 and 1834. Strickland was influenced by Greek architecture, as well as by the use of circular towers on exchange buildings in New York, Baltimore and London. His building has a semicircular portico and rotunda, with tall Corinthian columns, and is crowned by a slim tower, from which ships could be seen up and down the Delaware River. The tower recalls the Choragic Monument of Lysicrates, one of the most imitated monuments of antiquity.

Down below, the small, cobblestoned street in front, Dock Street, was the site of Dock Creek, which flowed to the river. It still flows to the Delaware, about eight feet below ground. The area around the Philadelphia Exchange and other buildings in Independence National Historical Park has undergone excavation to upgrade utility systems. The interior of the Exchange was renovated to house National Park Service offices.

5 Follow Dock Street or Walnut west to Third Street, turn right and walk a few steps to a reconstruction of a **watch box**, used by watchmen who guarded the buildings and kept a lookout for fires. A few steps further north is the former National Park Service's **Visitor Center (5)** (*Third Street between Chestnut and Walnut Streets*), which is used as park offices and storage since the 2001 opening of the **Independence Visitor Center** (*Sixth Street between Market and Arch Streets on Independence Mall*).

The old Visitor Center once displayed the Bicentennial Bell in a 130-foot bell tower. It was the British people's gift to America on its 200th anniversary of independence and is now in storage.

6 Across Third Street is the **First Bank of the United States (6)** (*Third Street between Chestnut and Walnut Streets*). It is the oldest bank building in the country and a superb example of Federal-style architecture. (Though the building is closed to the public, the exterior is a popular spot for photos.)

First Bank of the United States

Constructed between 1795 and 1797, the building was the headquarters of the government's bank until 1811, when its charter expired. The intricately carved American eagle on the tympanum of the pediment and the impressive, Greco-Roman look of the portico, with its leafy Corinthian capitals, lend the bank a certain grandeur and solidity, important features in the shaky early days of the republic. Stephen Girard, a French immigrant, wealthy merchant and shipowner who would later be known for his philanthropy, bought the building and used it for his Girard Bank from 1812 to 1831. After his death, the Girard National Bank occupied the building from 1832 to 1926. In 1955, it was obtained by the National Park Service, and it currently houses park offices.

7 A few steps away—on the southeast corner of Third and Chestnut—is the **Museum of the American Revolution (7)** (*101 South Third Street*), offering exhibits, recreated historical environments, as well as films and programs that immerse visitors in the Revolution. The museum, a popular tourist stop since its unveiling in 2017, is open from 10 a.m. to 5 p.m. daily and has extended summer hours from 9:30 a.m. to 6 p.m. daily.

At the entrance is the Declaration of Independence Plaza with a display of five cannons from the Revolutionary era. Inside the door, to your left, are statues of Aaron Burr, a Vice President of the United States, and Alexander Hamilton, the former U.S. Secretary of the Treasury, both posed as if firing pistols at one another, just as they did during their famous 1804 duel, resulting in Hamilton's death.

Head to the Lenfest Myer Theater for a film that delves into the background, experience and legacy of the Revolution. See an actual headquarters tent used by Gen. George Washington. Imagine the crucial, history-making decisions made there during the war for independence. In another area, view a scene of Americans tearing down an equestrian statue of King George III in New York City, and stand beneath the branches and lanterns of a life-size reproduction of the Boston Liberty Tree.

This museum is more than magnificent paintings and exhibits of relics telling the story of the Revolution. It involves you. It puts you on the receiving end of a British infantry charge at the Battle of Brandywine, and invites you to climb aboard a replica of a privateer ship where visitors learn about the war at sea. In one gallery, you can stand among life-size replicas of members of the Oneida Indian Nation and listen to the intense debate that led them to join the American cause. On the museum's lower level, children will especially enjoy four recreated historical environments: a military encampment, tavern, home and 18th-century meeting house. For a break, stop for refreshments at the Cross Keys Café on the first floor and visit the museum store for gifts inspired by the museum's artwork and artifacts.

❽ Returning to Third Street, walk south to encounter a charming, **18th-century-style garden (8)** (*Third and Walnut Streets*). It is on the site of the house of Dr. Benjamin Rush, a notable physician and 18th-century patriot. Benches are tucked away here amid the evergreens and holly.

❾ Begin strolling west on Walnut toward Fourth Street to reach the **Bishop White House (9)** (*309 Walnut Street*), the restored home of Pennsylvania's first Episcopal bishop and chaplain of the Continental Congress and United States Senate. The Right Rev. William White also served as rector of nearby Christ Church and St. Peter's Church. (At this writing, the house is closed to the public. When it is open, timed tickets are required for admission and must be obtained at the Independence Visitor Center on Independence Mall.)

Bishop White lived in the elegant brick house—midway between the two churches he served—from the time it was built in 1787 until his death in 1836. He is buried under the altar of Christ Church. His five children and 11 grandchildren played in the house's spacious, airy rooms. And many important men and women of the day, including Washington and Franklin, were entertained here. Ah, if walls could talk—what fascinating dinner conversations they could recount!

The house contains many furnishings, books and other items that belonged to the bishop, making it a treat for the history buff who wonders what life was like during the early days of the republic. The bishop's grandchildren commissioned John Sartain to paint a picture of his study, just as he left it at the time of his death. The painting, part of the portrait gallery in the **Second Bank of the United States,** was used later as a guide for restoring the room. One unusual feature of the house was an early version of the flush toilet, located off the kitchen.

Adjacent to the Bishop White House is a charming row of restored or reconstructed houses, occupied by the Friends of Independence

National Historical Park and the National Park Service, which uses space here as administrative offices. The house at 315 Walnut Street, built in 1793, was the home of Dr. William McIlvaine, a physician and surgeon. Across the street is the **Polish American Cultural Center** (*308 Walnut Street*), a museum and exhibit hall featuring Polish history and culture. Among the Polish heroes of the American Revolution were Thaddeus Kosciuszko, an engineer who designed the military fortifications for Philadelphia, West Point and Saratoga, and Count Casimir Pulaski, a general known as the "father of the American cavalry." (Open 10 a.m. to 4 p.m. Monday through Friday, from January to April, and Monday through Saturday from May to December. Admission is free. Gift shop open during exhibit hall hours.)

10 Walking further west on Walnut, look for a beautifully laid-out, **18th-century-style garden (10)** (*Walnut Street near Fourth Street*), recreated from one that was here in 1784. The meticulously kept flowers and shrubs adorn geometrically shaped beds and are changed with the seasons. At one end of the neat pathways is a summerhouse, beckoning walkers to rest on a bench and enjoy the view.

11 Exiting the garden, make your way to the **Todd House (11)** (*341 Walnut at Fourth Street*), a middle-class home built in 1775 by John Dilworth. (Currently closed to the public. When it is open, tickets are available at the Independence Visitor Center.)

The house has been restored to its 1790s appearance, when Quaker lawyer John Todd Jr. lived here with his wife, Dolley Payne Todd. He died during a yellow fever epidemic in 1793, and Dolley later married James Madison, who would become the fourth president of the United States. Stephen Moylan, a Revolutionary War general, lived here from 1796 to 1807. The house, which is furnished much as it was when the Todds lived here, is more modest than the Bishop White House, yet equally interesting because it is an example of a typical middle-class home of the period.

12 From the Todd House, walk north on Fourth Street, halfway to Chestnut. Turn right at an entranceway and follow the path leading to **Carpenters' Hall (12)** (*320 Chestnut Street*). The two-story, patterned, red-and-black brick building became an important setting in America's inexorable move toward independence. (Open 10 a.m. to 4 p.m. Tuesday through Sunday, closed on Tuesdays in January and February.)

Carpenters' Hall

The hall was erected between 1770 and 1773 by the Carpenters' Company, a building-trades guild founded in 1724 to support carpenters, who in those days were both architects and builders. It was a meeting place for George Washington, John Adams, Benjamin Franklin, Patrick Henry, Paul Revere, John Jay and others. And it hosted the First Continental Congress, whose delegates addressed a petition to King George III, detailing their grievances and asserting their rights and liberties. For about six weeks in September and October 1774, Carpenters' Hall was the stage for a great drama.

Following the dumping of tea in Boston Harbor by colonists protesting new taxes, the royal government had closed the port of Boston and garrisoned troops in the city. That, and other "intolerable acts," had enraged patriots throughout the colonies, who knew it could just as well have happened to them. So delegates from all of the colonies were invited to converge on Philadelphia, a metropolis of 30,000 that impressed them with the variety of its citizens' ethnic backgrounds and skills.

The scenes are easy to imagine, the delegates rising from Windsor chairs that are still in the hall to deliver fiery oratory. "Government is dissolved," declared Patrick Henry of Virginia. "Where are now your landmarks, your boundaries of colonies? . . . The distinctions between Virginians, Pennsylvanians, New Yorkers and New Englanders are no more. I am not a Virginian, but an American!" Cried New York lawyer John Jay, "We will never submit to be hewers of wood or drawers of water for any ministry or nation in the world!"

In the tasks that lay ahead, the delegates sought the help of God. The Rev. Jacob Duche, pastor of Christ Church, offered up the first prayer in Congress. His text was Psalm 35, part of which reads, "Plead thou my case, O Lord, with them that strive with me, and fight thou against them that fight against me."

At the time the Continental Congress met here, Carpenters' Hall was a plain meeting hall, with unfinished wood floors and fireplaces that were nothing more than crude cut-outs in the walls with hearths. Over the years, the Carpenters' Company, which still owns and operates the hall, couldn't resist the urge to make improvements, adding gilt, marble, tile and other adornments.

The First Bank of the United States once rented the building. Benjamin Franklin housed his Library Company here for a time. The American Philosophical Society rented part of the first floor for its scientific apparatus and astronomical instruments. The Franklin Institute leased space here, as did the Society for the Education of Female Children. And for many years, the C.J. Wolbert Auction Room, which sold everything from real estate to horses, made the hall its home. But in 1857 the Carpenters' Company decided to showcase its history and evicted the auctioneers.

Carpenters' Hall later was surrounded by ugly buildings and parking lots. But during the development of Independence National Historical Park, the area was cleared and the building became one of the park's great architectural centerpieces.

13 With Carpenters' Hall so much in demand from the beginning, the Carpenters' Company in 1790 erected **New Hall (13)** (*Chestnut Street east of Fourth Street, on the west side of Carpenters' Court*) to house its activities. The company wound up renting the first floor of New Hall to the United States War Department from 1791 to 1792, when Gen. Henry Knox served as President Washington's first secretary of war. (An interesting aside: The Continental Marine Corps was organized at the Tun Tavern in Philadelphia in 1775, and the U.S. Marine Corps was established by the U.S. Congress in Congress Hall in 1798.)

New Hall was razed in 1958 because of its rundown condition and reconstructed. It now serves as the **New Hall Military Museum (13)** and houses exhibits on the founding of the Marine Corps and Army and Navy Departments. (Currently open only for special events, such as Veterans Day weekend and Army/Navy Game weekend. Admission is free.)

Self-guiding exhibits include Revolutionary War weapons, uniforms and medals. "At no period of the naval history of the world, is it probable that marines were more important than during the War of the Revolution," wrote author James Fenimore Cooper.

14 At the entrance to Carpenters' Court is **Pemberton House (14)** (*316 Chestnut Street*), a reconstruction of the three-story brick home of Joseph Pemberton. A wealthy Quaker merchant, Pemberton was driven into bankruptcy when the Continental Congress restricted business dealings with England. His house, built in 1775, was sold at auction and later torn down in 1862. Rebuilt in the 1960s, it was used as the park's Army-Navy Museum. This handsome house, which is typical of the Georgian architecture of the 18th century, now functions as an "America's National Parks" store, selling books and souvenirs.

15 Leaving Pemberton House, cross Chestnut Street to the **National Liberty Museum (15)** (*321 Chestnut Street*), four floors of exhibits and glass art that explore liberty as a human quest. (Open seven days a week; hours change according to the season.) See the 21-foot "Flame of Liberty," a stunning glass flame exhibit by Dale Chihuly. The Flame Gallery, completely renovated in 2018, provides a 360-degree experience of inspirational words, images and sounds. At the end of the presentation, touch the surrounding ring and watch the flame erupt in bright colors. Nearby, visit a gallery with stained-glass Biblical scenes by Maurice Gareau and remember the colonists who came to America for religious freedom. Also, see the interactive mirror exhibit, original White House china in Liberty Hall, and displays of glass art and handmade jewelry.

16 A few steps from the museum is a small alley, Orianna Street, which leads to **Franklin Court (16)** (*Market Street between Third and Fourth Streets*). (Exhibits are open 9 a.m. to 5 p.m. daily. Rest rooms are available.)

Towering steel frames, rising from a slate base, outline the general dimensions of Benjamin Franklin's three-story brick house. It was here that Franklin died on April 17, 1790, at 84, after an illustrious career as diplomat, author, inventor, builder and newspaper publisher. The steel skeleton, designed by architect Robert Venturi, was erected in 1976, after it was determined that not enough was known about Franklin's house to build an accurate reconstruction.

The brick house was the only home Franklin ever owned. It was, he said, "a good House contrived to my Mind." Construction began in 1763, and two years later Franklin's wife, Deborah, moved in while her husband was in London, serving as Pennsylvania's representative to the crown. Franklin built an addition to his three-story house in 1786.

He was feeble during his last few years in Philadelphia and was unable to stand without pain. But he continued to serve the nation at the Constitutional Convention in 1787 and rejoiced over the country's successes. His daughter, Sarah Bache, remained close during his declining final days. "My malady renders my sitting up to write rather painful to me," he wrote George Washington on September 16, 1789. "But I cannot let my son-in-law, Mr. Bache, part for New York without congratulating you by him . . . on the growing strength of our new government under your administration. For my personal ease I should have died two years ago; but, though those years have been spent in excruciating pain, I am pleased that I have lived them, since they have brought me to see our present situation."

Franklin's final public act was affixing his name to a memorial to Congress recommending the dissolution of the slavery system. As he lay dying at home, his daughter advised him to change his position in bed so he could breathe more easily. "A dying man can do nothing easy," Franklin told her, then passed away. A huge funeral procession of 20,000 people gathered at Independence Hall to honor his memory.

Bache died at the Franklin home in 1808, and her heirs leased the house to a succession of tenants until 1812, when it was sold and demolished to make way for commercial development.

17 Beneath the site of Franklin's home is a unique **underground Benjamin Franklin Museum (17)** detailing the life and impressive contributions of Philadelphia's leading citizen. Paintings, inventions, a film and artifacts recall Franklin's life. The artifacts include his desk, a library chair-ladder and a Franklin stove. You can also see Franklin's family Bible, a reproduction of his famous glass harmonica and an antique sedan chair like the one he used.

18 Returning to ground level, walk across the courtyard and pass through a carriageway to the **Market Street Houses (18)** *(316, 318, 320 Market Street)*, restorations of 18th-century buildings fronting on Market Street. Franklin had three houses built shortly after his return from France to be used as rental properties. Today they contain an 18th-century printing office, an architectural-cultural exhibit and an operating U.S. post office.

The print shop, 320 Market, is devoted to Franklin's days as a printer, the trade he pursued when he first arrived in Philadelphia as a lad of 17. An adjacent house, 318 Market, contains the architectural/archaeological exhibit showing Franklin's interest in building and in fire prevention. At 316 Market, a post office with a colonial theme, commemorative stamps are sold and letters are canceled with the postmark "B. Free Franklin," which was made famous by the nation's best-known postmaster.

19 Walk west on Market to Fourth Street, turn left and head south to Chestnut, where you will find the **Second Bank of the United States (19)** *(420 Chestnut between Fourth and Fifth Streets)*, a repository of many fine paintings. (The bank is open 11 a.m. to 5 p.m. Saturdays and Sundays; check for winter hours.)

This handsome building with Doric columns was based on the Parthenon. Second Bank President Nicholas Biddle held a design competition for the building, with one requirement: architects had to use the Greek style. The bank, designed by William Strickland, was built between 1819 and 1824 and is one of the finest examples of Greek Revival architecture in the nation. Inside are intricate barrel-vaulted ceilings above Ionic colonnades.

The bank was at the center of a constitutional controversy between Biddle and President Andrew Jackson, who vetoed a bill to renew its charter, putting the bank out of business in 1836. Jackson challenged the constitutionality of a national bank and the bank's monopolistic influence on the nation's economy. A bank—this one under Pennsylvania charter—continued at the location until 1841. When Charles Dickens looked at the Second Bank on the night of his arrival that

Second Bank of the United States

year, he saw "a handsome building of white marble, which had a mournful ghost-like aspect." The federal government purchased the building about 1845, using it as the Custom House until 1934. It is still popularly known in the city as "the old Custom House."

Though no longer keeping money, the Second Bank does hold a treasure: Independence National Park's portrait gallery. Called the "People of Independence," it is a collection of more than 100 paintings of colonial and federal leaders, most of them painted by Charles Willson Peale. Peale, who lived from 1741 to 1827, had sought to record and preserve images of the leaders of the Revolution. These paintings were shown as part of Peale's private "Gallery of Illustrious Personages," which opened in the 1780s. The City of Philadelphia purchased many of the portraits after the artist's death. Among the gallery's paintings are ones of Washington and his wife, Martha; Franklin; Jefferson; James Madison and his wife, Dolley; John Adams; and John Paul Jones.

㉟ As you leave the Second Bank, walk west on Chestnut, then through the passageway to the right of the bank to cobblestoned Library Street. On your right is **Library Hall (20)** (*105 South*

Fifth Street near Chestnut), a 20th-century reconstruction of Benjamin Franklin's Library Company of Philadelphia, the oldest subscription library in the United States. (Open by appointment.)

Library Hall now houses the library of the American Philosophical Society, founded by Franklin in 1743. It contains Franklin's books and papers, along with the original journals of the Lewis and Clark expedition and a copy of the Declaration of Independence in Thomas Jefferson's handwriting. Members of the library included Washington, Jefferson, Thomas Paine, Alexander Hamilton, John Adams and the Marquis de Lafayette.

The original building was erected between 1785 and 1789 to house the collections of the Library Company, which had been founded in 1731 by Franklin and his friends. Members could read at the library or borrow books. Indeed, delegates to the Continental Congress and the Constitutional Convention used this book repository—making it a forerunner of the Library of Congress. The library, a building of stately design by William Thornton, who later designed the Capitol in Washington, D.C., was demolished in 1884 and rebuilt by the American Philosophical Society in 1959. Though the building is larger, its Fifth Street facade looks exactly as it did in 1789—right down to the statue of Franklin, dressed in classic garb, in the niche above the doorway. The original Franklin statue can be seen in a sidewalk display window at the Library Company of Philadelphia in the 1300 block of Locust Street.

㉑ Across from the Fifth Street entrance to Library Hall is **Philosophical Hall (21)** (*104 South Fifth Street near Chestnut Street on Independence Square*), a brick building with marble trim. Constructed between 1785 and 1789, it is the headquarters of the American Philosophical Society, founded in 1743 and the oldest learned society in the United States. (Philosophical Hall provides space for APS offices and houses a museum that is open to the public from 10 a.m. to 5 p.m. Thursday through Sunday, from April to December each year.)

This internationally renowned organization was founded by Franklin to seek "useful knowledge" and has served as a kind of think tank for the United States. Its members have included John Audubon, Charles Darwin, Thomas Edison, Louis Pasteur, Madame Marie Curie and Robert Frost and, currently, former President Barack Obama, author Eric Foner and actor John Lithgow. Membership is by invitation only, through the nomination of current mem-

Philosophical Hall

bers, of whom there are about 700 at any given time. The competition is tough: This century, about 200 members have won the Nobel Prize.

22 Leaving Philosophical Hall, walk north on Fifth Street, passing the elegant Bourse building (*between Chestnut and Market*) with its Food Hall and shops. Turn left on Market Street and walk a few steps to **Independence Visitor Center (22)** (*Sixth Street between Market and Arch*), where you'll be greeted by park rangers in Smokey-Bear hats and get oriented for the final leg of your walk. (Open 8:30 a.m. to 6 p.m.)

The slender brick building—with its two-story-high windows—shows a free 28-minute film, "Independence," and has exhibits, a cafe and information kiosks with videos, brochures and maps. Here you can obtain free, timed tickets to tour Independence Hall as well as tickets to more than 100 other area tours and attractions. A gift shop and rest rooms are located near the entrance.

The building houses the Philadelphia Visitor Center (*Sixth Street between Market and Arch*), which offers free literature on the city and help with personalized itineraries. (A new attraction—the Faith and

Liberty Discovery Center, which traces the impact of the Bible on America—is being developed by the American Bible Society just east of the visitor center at Fifth and Market Streets. It is expected to open by the end of 2020.)

㉓ Almost next door to the Visitor Center is the **National Constitution Center (23)** (*525 Arch Street, Independence Mall North*), which offers an interactive tour of American democracy. Walk north on Sixth Street and cross over Arch Street. (Open 9:30 a.m. to 5 p.m. Monday through Saturday, and 12 p.m. to 5 p.m. on Sunday. Admission $14.50 for adults; $13 for seniors over 65 and college students with ID; $11 for youths 6 to 18 and military veterans, and free for children up to 5 and active military service members.)

The center's mission is to increase understanding of the Constitution and its relevance to our lives. Visitors pass through DeVos Hall, where they will see "The Story of We the People," a permanent exhibit that includes 18th-century artifacts unearthed during the center's construction. They can then enter the Kimmel Theater, an unusual 350-seat star-shaped theater showing "Freedom Rising," a 17-minute production combining film, a live actor and video projection on a 360-degree screen.

After the show, visit the main exhibit space in the center, with displays of artifacts and more than 100 interactive and multimedia elements.

One of the high points is Signers' Hall, where visitors can walk among 42 life-size bronze statues of the 39 men who signed the Con-

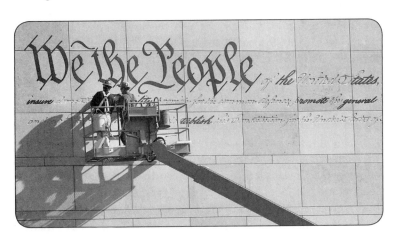

The National Constitution Center

stitution and three who dissented. Before leaving, sign your name to the Constitution, a custom-made signing book. You can also sign as a dissenter and explain your reasons. Displayed in an alcove adjacent to Signers' Hall is a rare original copy of the first public printing of the Constitution, published in *The Pennsylvania Packet and Daily Advertiser* on September 19, 1787, by John Dunlap and David Claypoole. There are only about 25 known copies of this printing in the world. This treasured document is periodically given a rest because of its age and replaced with a high-resolution facsimile.

24 Exit the National Constitution Center and retrace your footsteps. Head south on Sixth Street, east on Market Street, then south on Fifth Street toward Independence Hall (*Chestnut Street between Fifth and Sixth Streets*), where you will pass through a security checkpoint before visiting **Old City Hall (24)** (*Fifth and Chestnut Streets*), once home of the U.S. Supreme Court. (Open daily, 9 a.m. to 5 p.m.)

This box-like brick building was constructed between 1789 and 1791 and originally was intended to serve the municipal government. But when Philadelphia became the temporary capital of the nation, the building was offered to the federal government. The Supreme Court met here from 1791 to 1800, with John Jay presiding as the nation's first chief justice. During the same period, the building served as headquarters for volunteers fighting yellow fever outbreaks. The first floor focuses on the Supreme Court's stay here. Most of the furnishings are from the period but not original to the room. After the national government moved to Washington, the structure was converted to a City Hall and also was used by the Philadelphia courts during the 19th century. City offices made a gradual move to the new City Hall erected at Broad and Market Streets shortly before the turn of the 20th century.

25 Now, walk next door to the most imposing building on Independence Square, **Independence Hall (25)** (*Chestnut Street between Fifth and Sixth Streets*), where the United States was born. In the Pennsylvania Assembly Room, delegates from the 13 colonies adopted the Declaration of Independence, the Articles of Confederation and the federal Constitution. (The hall is open from 9 a.m. to 5 p.m. daily. Free tickets are available on the morning of your visit at the Independence Visitor Center, or you can reserve them in advance online at recreation.gov, or by calling 877-444-6777. Visitors

Independence
Hall

are admitted, by tour only, on a first-come, first-served basis. Tours
begin in the East Wing, and visitors should arrive 30 minutes before
the scheduled tour time. Pamphlets are available in Chinese, French,
German, Hebrew, Italian, Japanese, Spanish and Russian.)

Outside the hall are two bronze plaques in the pavement along
Chestnut Street. One marks the place where President-elect Abraham Lincoln stood on February 22, 1861—Washington's birthday—
when he raised the American flag. It had 34 stars then, the last one
for Kansas, which had just been admitted to the Union after fierce
fighting over the issue of slavery. Standing near Lincoln was one of
Philadelphia's most popular military units, the Washington Grays,
looking smart in epaulets and crisp gray uniforms. They raised their
muskets high and fired a salute. "As the sun just rising kissed the
quivering folds of the national emblem, a cheer arose from thousands of loyal throats that was an earnest of unflinching devotion of
the City of Brotherly Love," wrote a member of the Grays. When the
Civil War broke out a few weeks later, recruits flocked to the Grays.
President Lincoln returned in 1865—to lie in state in Independence
Hall after his assassination.

The other plaque in front of Independence Hall marks the spot
where John F. Kennedy stood when he delivered a speech on July 4,
1962. A statue of George Washington, erected in 1869, stands nearby.

Independence Hall

Independence Hall was constructed between 1732 and 1756 to serve as the new State House of the Province of Pennsylvania. Its designer, Andrew Hamilton, an eminent lawyer and speaker of the Pennsylvania Assembly, had no idea of the much bigger role his building would play in history. (Some historians say the honor for the design belongs to Edmund Woolley, a master carpenter.)

Here, a group of extraordinary men took hold of their destiny and the destiny of generations to come. The Second Continental Congress met here from 1775 to 1783 (except for the winter of 1777–78, when the British occupied the city). George Washington was appointed commander-in-chief of the Continental Army here. And independence was proclaimed here by representatives of the 13 colonies.

In this elegant structure, the design of the American flag was adopted. The first foreign minister to the United States—France's Conrad Alexandre Gérard—was received. The news of the British defeat and surrender at Yorktown, Virginia, was reported. And delegates found a way of distributing powers between the local and national governments, first with the Articles of Confederation, then with the Constitution.

Walk into the entrance hall. To the left is the **Pennsylvania Assembly Room**, looking much as it looked when the founders met here. Though most of the original furniture was destroyed during the British occupation, the room is filled with period pieces—and two originals. The **silver inkstand** on the president's desk is the one used by the delegates to sign the Declaration of Independence and the Constitution. And the **"rising sun" chair** used by Washington as he presided during the Constitutional Convention is an original. Visitors can easily imagine the patriots dipping their quills into the inkstand and scratching their names to the parchment.

Here, after much debate and consideration, the colonies declared their independence. Thomas Jefferson wrote the draft of the document, and with modifications by John Adams and Benjamin Franklin, it was adopted by Congress on July 4, 1776. John Hancock, president of the Congress, called on all members to sign it to show strong unanimity. "There must be no pulling different ways: We must all hang together," he said. Franklin reportedly agreed, adding, "We must indeed all hang together, or most assuredly we shall all hang separately." When Jefferson was dying in the summer of 1826, his mind turned back to that time. His last words were: "Is it the Fourth?" (It was. Jefferson and John Adams died the same day, July 4, 1826.)

When delegates gathered here in 1787 to seek agreement on a new Constitution, once again the stakes were high. Edmund Randolph, governor of Virginia, said that local politicians would oppose any system that reduced their own power. "They will not cherish the great oak which is to reduce them to paltry shrubs," he said.

Pennsylvania Assembly Room at Independence Hall

As the new government began to take shape, delegates were not sure whether the people would accept their work either. James Madison saw the young nation at a crossroads. "If the present moment be lost, it is hard to say what may be our fate," he said.

In the end, the Federalists who favored the new Constitution prevailed. A committee was appointed to write a final draft of the document, which began with a preamble: "We, the people of the United States, in order to form a more perfect Union, establish justice, insure domestic tranquility, provide for the common defense, promote the general welfare, and secure the blessings of liberty to ourselves and our posterity, do ordain and establish this Constitution for the United States of America."

After four months of debate and wrangling over details, the delegates dipped their quills in the silver inkstand that had been designed by Philip Syng in 1752 for the Pennsylvania Assembly and affixed their signatures on the parchment. George Washington, president of the convention, signed first. Elbridge Gerry of Massachusetts and Edmund Randolph and George Mason, both of Virginia, refused to sign. Benjamin Franklin reportedly shed tears as he put his name on the document.

Afterward, Franklin's eyes fell on the convention president's dignified wooden chair, decorated on the back with the carving of a sun half-hidden by the horizon. Painters have "found it difficult to distinguish in their art a rising from a setting sun," said the old man. "I have often, and often in the course of the session and the vicissitudes of my hopes and fears as to its issue, looked at that behind the president without being able to tell whether it was rising or setting. But now at length I have the happiness to know that it is a rising, and not a setting sun."

Across the hall from the Assembly Room is the chamber of the **Pennsylvania Supreme Court**, with buff-colored walls and the state's handsome coat-of-arms above the judge's bench. (It replaced the coat-of-arms of King George III, which was ripped from the wall and burned after the first reading of the Declaration of Independence on July 8, 1776.) Here, where the laws of England once were enforced, the prisoner's dock and jury box stand empty, as if court had just recessed. An interesting feature of the room is the small boxes on the floor. The room had no fireplaces, so boxes containing live coals helped warm the feet.

On the second floor, as you enter the anteroom, look to the left to see the **Governor's Council Chamber**, the office where Proprietary

Governor John Penn administered the business of Pennsylvania's colonial government. Beyond the anteroom is the airy, 100-foot-long **Long Gallery**. It served as a banquet room for the fledgling republic, as a prison for American officers during the British occupation, and as a museum of natural history and portraiture when Charles Willson Peale rented it from 1802 to 1828. Next to the Long Gallery is the **Committee of the Assembly's Chamber**, where the Pennsylvania government met while the Continental Congress used its assembly room.

Over more than two centuries, presidents and other distinguished visitors have come to Independence Hall. In 1861, President-elect Abraham Lincoln said, "I am filled with deep emotion at finding myself standing in this place, where were collected together the wisdom, the patriotism, the devotion to principle, from which sprang the institutions under which we live. . . . All the political sentiments I entertain have been drawn, so far as I have been able to draw them, from sentiments which originated and were given to the world from this Hall. I have never had a feeling politically that did not spring from the sentiments embodied in the Declaration of Independence."

26 Leave Independence Hall from the south door and walk out onto **Independence Square (26)**, the former State House Yard (*between Chestnut and Walnut Streets and Fifth and Sixth Streets*), where the Declaration of Independence was first read.

The Liberty Bell and all the bells of the city rang continuously that day in celebration. Philadelphians once came here for demonstrations and mass meetings. Today, it is a lovely, tree-shaded park. A statue of Commodore John Barry, an Irish-born Philadelphian who became the father of the United States Navy, stands at an intersection of pathways in the square.

Across from the square, on the southeast corner of Walnut and Sixth Streets, once stood the infamous Walnut Street Prison, where Tories, debtors, felons and prisoners-of-war were held before being taken to the State House for trial. Robert Morris, financier of the Revolution, was incarcerated between 1798 and 1801 in a debtor's lockup behind the jail.

Opposite the square's southwest corner is **Washington Square**, one of William Penn's five planned squares and the unmarked burial ground for thousands of Revolutionary War soldiers. As you walk back across Independence Square toward Chestnut Street, gaze up at the great clock on the west wall of Independence Hall. The original was set in place in 1752 and removed in 1828. The National Park Service replaced it in 1972 with a 14-foot carved replica.

27 Move now through the arches connecting Independence Hall and **Congress Hall (27)** (*Sixth and Chestnut Streets*), where the newly formed United States Congress convened between 1790 and 1800 while the Capitol in Washington was being erected. (Open daily by tour only from 9 a.m. to 5 p.m. Visitors are admitted free, on a first-come, first-served basis. Audio tapes are available in Chinese, French, German, Italian, Japanese, Russian and Spanish.)

The building was constructed between 1787 and 1789 and is a fine example of late Georgian architecture. Though originally designed to serve as the Philadelphia County Court House, it played a far greater role in the early days of the nation. Many historic debates took place in the **House of Representatives Chamber** on the first floor and the **Senate Chamber** upstairs. Washington was inaugurated for his second term as president in this building, and John Adams was sworn in as the country's second president. The Second

Congress Hall

Bank of the United States, Federal Mint and Department of the Navy were established here. And the John Jay Treaty with England was debated and ratified here.

The building later was used for federal and local courts. It was abandoned in 1895 and fell into disrepair but subsequently was restored as a historic landmark. With its handsome fanlight over the door, plaster ceiling beading, 18th-century eagle fresco and many original furnishings, the hall has become one of the great historic attractions in the park.

28 Now walk one block west to Seventh Street, cross Chestnut and continue a half block north to the former **Philadelphia History Museum (28)** (*15 South Seventh Street*), which told the Philadelphia story from its earliest beginnings to the present—until its operation was suspended in the summer of 2018. It is not clear when or if it will reopen, but the location is worthy of note.

The small museum was founded in 1938 by radio entrepreneur Atwater Kent. The Greek Revival building, designed by John Haviland, was built between 1825 and 1827. Inside, visitors saw maps on the city's development and exhibits, dioramas and memorabilia on municipal services, manufacturing, shipbuilding and popular culture.

29 Continue north to Market Street, then cross over Seventh Street to the **Graff House**, also known as **Declaration House (29)** (*Seventh and Market Streets*). Here is the reconstructed house of Jacob Graff Jr., where Thomas Jefferson lived when he drafted the Declaration of Independence. (Currently closed to the public.)

The original brick building was constructed by Graff in 1775 and was typically Georgian, with fireplaces in many rooms. It changed hands over the years, even serving time as a printer's shop before being razed in 1883. In its place the Penn National Bank erected a new building designed by architect Frank Furness. The bank was demolished during the Depression and was replaced by Sam Besses' Tom Thumb Luncheonette. The Philadelphia Convention and Visitors Bureau wanted the Graff House back, and $2 million was set aside in 1968 to rebuild it. Two stone lintels salvaged from the demolition were used in the reconstruction in 1975.

Jefferson was a 33-year-old delegate from Virginia to the Continental Congress in 1776 when he rented two furnished second-floor rooms here, seeking a little peace and quiet. Congress had antici-

Declaration
House

pated a favorable vote on independence and placed Jefferson, Benjamin Franklin, John Adams, Robert R. Livingston and Roger Sherman on a committee to prepare a declaration. Jefferson labored over the draft, writing and rewriting it. "At the time of writing that instrument I was lodged in the house of a Mr. Gratz [Graff], a new brick house, three stories high, of which I rented the second floor . . . ," Jefferson wrote. "In that parlor I wrote habitually, and in it wrote that paper particularly."

When open, the first floor of the Graff House has offered exhibits and a brief film on the drafting process. The second floor has a bedroom and parlor, filled with period furnishings similar to those Jefferson would have used. They have included reproductions of Jefferson's swivel chair and the lap desk he used when he wrote the declaration.

30 When you leave Graff House, head east on Market Street to Sixth Street, the site of the **President's House (30)** (*Market and Sixth Streets*), where two founding fathers lived and worked while serving as president—George Washington from 1790 to 1797 and John Adams from 1797 to 1800. The elegant three-story mansion that once stood here is now marked by an open-air pavilion with brick walls and architectural features to outline the area of the original building. The site also displays some original foundations of the property that Washington called the "the best single house in the city." But the story of this historic site would be incomplete without also commemorating the roles of Washington's slaves in the household and in American society. The memorial—dubbed **"President's House: Freedom and Slavery in the Making of a New Nation"**— uses signage and video exhibits to reveal the lives of slaves who toiled at the executive mansion. At least nine were brought from Washington's Mount Vernon home in Virginia to serve at the executive mansion—steps away from Independence Hall where the Declaration of Independence announced the "self-evident" truth that "all Men are created equal."

31 Adjacent to the President's House is the last stop of our walk: the **Liberty Bell Center (31)** (*Fifth Street near Chestnut Street, facing Independence Hall; GPS is 526 Market Street*). (The building that houses one of the nation's most cherished symbols is open 9 a.m. to 5 p.m. seven days a week, with extended hours in summer.)

The Liberty Bell was originally cast to mark the 50th anniversary of the Pennsylvania Charter of Privileges, the democratic constitution that William Penn granted his colony in 1701. The guarantees of freedom and liberty were commemorated when the bell was ordered in 1751 with this inscription, chosen from Leviticus in the Old Testament: "Proclaim liberty throughout all the land, unto all the inhabitants thereof."

The bell was cast in the Whitechapel Foundry in London in 1751 and either developed a crack en route to Philadelphia or cracked soon after its arrival. It was melted down by local brass founders, recast and hung in the State House tower, where it rang out for important meetings, fire alarms and special events. Over the years, the tower deteriorated, and a 1774 account contended that "they are afraid to ring the bell, lest by doing so the steeple should fall down."

The bell's most dramatic role came on July 8, 1776, when it reportedly was tolled to bring Philadelphians to the State House Yard, where the Declaration of Independence was first read publicly. The bell may or may not have rung out that day, but other bells in the city did. The story of the ringing of the State House bell "to proclaim liberty throughout the land" originated with and was popularized by the 19th-century Philadelphia writer George Lippard. When the British Army entered Philadelphia in 1777, the bell was hustled to safety near Allentown, to prevent its being melted down for cannon.

The bell cracked again in the first half of the 19th century—tradition says while tolling for the funeral of Chief Justice John Marshall in 1835. It was last formally rung on Washington's birthday in 1846. The abolitionist movement used the bell, and its inscription, as a symbol and coined the term "Liberty Bell."

What better way to end a walk through our earliest history as a nation than by paying respects to this most famous cracked bell?

"North of Market"

"North of Market"

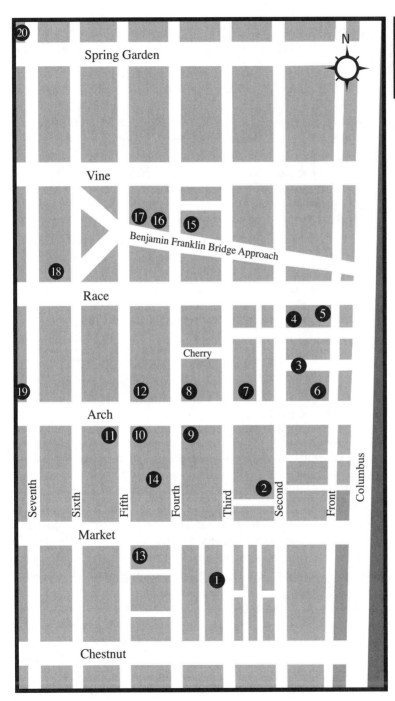

USEFUL INFORMATION

Visitors will find a wide array of restaurants for any taste and budget. They include Fork Restaurant, 306 Market Street; the Continental Restaurant and Martini Bar, 138 Market Street; Benton's Bar and Grill, Fourth and Arch Streets; and the Food Hall at the Bourse, Fifth Street near Chestnut.

Public parking is available at an underground facility on Fifth Street between Market and Arch Streets, on Seventh Street between Chestnut and Market Streets, and on Second Street between Chestnut and Walnut Streets. Signs also direct visitors to other public parking lots.

With the limited parking, you may want to use public transportation. SEPTA buses and the Market Street subway provide good alternatives to driving.

Walkers who want to get off their feet for a while may enjoy a horse-drawn carriage or motorized, Victorian-style trolley, both of which serve Old City as well as other historic neighborhoods.

Introduction

Philadelphia takes on a different look north of Market Street. The rich historic houses, elegant Georgian architecture and manicured National Park grounds are largely gone here. In colonial days, this area was the rough, working side of town, a place of great commerce and industry, with bustling wharves and warehouses. The people here were craftsmen and artisans. They earned less, lived in modest houses and frequented waterfront taverns. Thus, in the 18th century, the folks living "north of Market" were often considered less socially acceptable than the more affluent city dwellers further south.

No need to speak of them in whispers anymore. Today, this venerable neighborhood—generally extending from Market to Vine Street and Front to Fifth Street—is called "Old City" and is one of the most visited areas of Philadelphia. It takes in Elfreth's Alley, Loxley Court, the Betsy Ross House, Franklin Square (one of William Penn's original squares) and several places of worship, reflecting the city's diverse religious life. Christ Church, the Free Quaker Meeting House and Congregation Mikveh Israel are here, along with fine museums and old burial grounds.

Benjamin Franklin built his home on Market between Third and Fourth Streets, on the border of the area. He was often seen walking the streets, sometimes in the company of George Washington and John Adams. Imagine these giants—some of the world's most progressive thinkers—taking a stroll in the city. But why not? Presidents Washington and Adams also lived on the boundary of Old City—in Philadelphia's "White House," a red brick executive mansion (no longer standing but marked by a memorial) at Sixth and Market Streets. All three—Franklin, Washington and Adams—crossed "north of Market" to attend services at Christ Church, joining many other notables of the day.

The imprint of their time remains with us today, sometimes out in the open, sometimes tucked away on a narrow street, down a brick pathway and through an ornate iron gate. Look for the little reminders of the past, such as the stepping stone outside of Christ Church, where ladies and gentlemen stepped down from their carriages, or the stone troughs in Fairmount Park, where horses stopped to drink.

Though some buildings are historical reproductions, what you see across Philadelphia is largely original—original houses, churches, banks and community halls. And gardens. There is no greater delight, in the honking blare of the city, than to come upon one of these quiet eddies, a formal herb garden in a walled courtyard or an ancient trellis dripping wisteria off a back porch. For this is still a city of neighborhoods, where rowhouse residences coexist with houses of commerce.

Several facilities should make the tour of this area more enjoyable: the **Independence Visitor Center** (*Sixth Street between Market and Arch Streets*), the **Liberty Bell Center** (*Sixth and Chestnut Streets*) and the **National Constitution Center** (*Sixth and Arch Streets*).

The Tour

❶ Using **Independence Mall** as a starting point, walk east on Market Street toward the Delaware River. Make a brief stop at the former **Norwegian Seamen's Church (1)** (*Third Street near Market Street*), a Greek Revival building that has been used as a bank, church and restaurant-bar since its construction in 1837.

This classic structure was designed by architect William Strickland, who loved the Greek Revival style and employed pillars liberally in his work. Here, he placed four huge Corinthian columns atop a flight of granite steps. Other Strickland structures include the Philadelphia Exchange, the Second Bank of the United States and the steeple of Independence Hall, designed for its 1828 restoration (all of them stops on Walk 1).

The old seamen's church began as a financial institution, serving as the Mechanics Bank (until 1904), the Citizens Bank (until 1921) and the State Bank of Pennsylvania (1921–23). The building was dedicated as the Norwegian Seamen's Church in 1931 and was frequented by men from ships that steamed into Philadelphia, one of the busiest ports on the East Coast. Sailors often were seen standing and chatting on its steps. The site now houses a bar and restaurant. After more than a century and a half, the building still carries a certain dignity.

2 Cross over Market, head east about a block and look for the slender white spire atop **Christ Church (2)** (*Second and Church Streets near Market*), one of the most revered and beautiful 18th-century structures in the nation.

Called the "Nation's Church" because so many patriots worshipped here, it was designated a national shrine by an act of Congress and has been celebrated for its historical, architectural and religious significance. (Open 9 a.m. to 5 p.m. Monday to Saturday, and 12:30 p.m. to 5 p.m. on Sunday. It serves an active Episcopal parish with services at 9 and 11 a.m. on Sunday and at noon on Wednesdays.)

The congregation of Christ Church claims a veritable *Who's Who* of American history. The Second Continental Congress worshipped here as a body in 1775 and 1776. Fifteen signers of the Declaration of Independence attended services here. Brass plaques mark the pews reserved for George Washington and his family (Pew 58), Benjamin Franklin (Pew 70), Betsy Ross (Pew 12) and the Penn family, who by 1776 were no longer Quakers (Pew 60). Other worshippers included John Adams and Thomas Jefferson. Though not a particularly devout man, Franklin saw the benefits of religious beliefs and church attendance. In a letter to Thomas Paine, he once reasoned that "if men are so wicked *with religion*, what would they be *if without it*?"

The stately Georgian church, with its arched windows and classic symmetry, was built between 1727 and 1744 and immediately

Christ Church

became one of the city's great treasures. Once considered the most sumptuous building in North America, it was designed by vestryman and physician John Kearsley and replaced a smaller church built in 1695. The towering steeple, which rises 200 feet, was completed in 1754 and was partially financed by Franklin and the Penn family. Franklin also is said to have had a hand in the design of the addition. The church spire, long reputed to be the tallest in the colonies, dominated the city skyline and was one of the first landmarks sighted by people arriving by ship. When the British occupied Philadelphia in 1777, the bells in the tower were removed to prevent them from falling into enemy hands and being cast into cannon. Those same bells rang throughout the day on July 4, 1788, when 10 of the 13 states agreed to ratify the Constitution.

In the churchyard are the graves of two signers of the Declaration of Independence—Robert Morris and James Wilson—and a signer of the Constitution, Pierce Butler. Gen. Charles Lee, who was court-martialed in 1778 for his retreat at the Battle of Monmouth Court House and disrespect shown to Washington, also is buried here. Benches in the yard and in the small adjacent park at Second and Market Streets provide rest stops for weary sightseers.

Inside the church is a 600-year-old mahogany baptismal font, from which William Penn was baptized in England, where his family belonged to the Anglican Church. It was built by Welsh craftsmen and given to Christ Church by the Bishop of London. At the front of the church, to the right of the altar, is a President's Door, used by Washington and other visiting dignitaries. The wineglass-shaped pulpit was built in 1770 by John Folwell, who also crafted the handsome "rising sun" chair used by George Washington at Independence Hall.

Bishop William White, whose home we visited in Walk 1, preached from this pulpit from 1779 to 1836. He is buried nearby, under the altar. On an upcoming stop, we will visit Christ Church Burial Ground, three blocks west of the church on Fifth Street.

❸ Leaving Christ Church, walk north on Second Street to one of Philadelphia's most charming historic sites, **Elfreth's Alley (3)** (*extending from Second to Front Street, between Arch and Race Streets*). This is the oldest continuously occupied residential street in the United States. Homeowners celebrate Fete Days in early June and open their homes to tours hosted by guides in colonial dress. Many of the houses also are open in December for Christmas tours. (For ticket information and reservations, call the Elfreth's Alley Association at 215-574-0560 or go to www.elfrethsalley.org.) The rest of the year, the public can tour a restored colonial dressmaker's home at No. 126, called the Mantua Maker's Museum House, and the Windsor Chairmaker's House at No. 124. (The alley is open 12 to 5 p.m. daily. An admission charge of $3 for adults and $2 for children covers walk-through tours of the museum during the season, generally running from March to December. Also, 45-minute guided tours of the alley and museum are offered at 1 p.m. on Fridays and at 1 p.m. and 3 p.m. on Saturdays and Sundays. The charge is $8 for adults and $2 for children from age 5 to 12. Tickets can be purchased in advance or at the museum before a tour. Private group tours are available throughout the year.)

A walk down Elfreth's Alley, with its cobblestoned street and narrow rowhouses, is a walk into Philadelphia's past. On this block-long

Elfreth's Alley

street, which has been occupied continuously since 1713, it is easy to imagine a time when these 33 colonial and Federal-style houses were lived in by printers, carpenters, cabinetmakers, pewterers, silversmiths—and a blacksmith, Jeremiah Elfreth, for whom the street is named. Other houses were occupied by ship captains and workers who depended on the shipping industry.

The Elfreth's Alley Association has restored Nos. 124 and 126. The Windsor Chairmaker's House, No. 124, dates to 1755. Here, you can see the skill it took to create the chairs that were so popular during the period. No. 126 belonged to two dressmakers, who made mantuas, cape-like cloaks popular during the 18th century. Houses along the street date to between 1728 and 1836. The oldest are two-and-a-half story structures; the three-and-a-half story houses were built after the Revolutionary War and show influences of the Federal style.

Residents are largely accustomed to the steady stream of tourists snapping pictures of the houses. Occasionally someone will invite visitors inside for a tour. The properties here do not generally stay in one family and get passed on from one generation to the next. The block, though historic, is part of a working community. Young professionals, architects, artists and other creative people move into the small houses but move on as their families increase in size.

❹ Returning to Second Street, turn right and stroll a few steps to the **Fireman's Hall Museum (4)** (*147 North Second Street*). This is an authentic turn-of-the-century (1902) firehouse that tells the story of fire-fighting in Philadelphia—from the organization of the first fire department by Benjamin Franklin in 1736 to the professional departments of today. (Open 10 a.m. to 4 p.m. Tuesday through Saturday; closed Sundays, Mondays and holidays. Admission is free.)

The museum is an especially appropriate stop in Philadelphia—the place William Penn planned to be a "Greene Country Towne, which will never be burnt, and allways be wholsome." The building was constructed as the headquarters of the city's Engine Company, which traces its history to Franklin's Union Fire Company and is thus the oldest active fire company in the United States. The museum exhibits rare and beautiful pieces of fire apparatus in use between 1731 and 1907, including hand- and horse-drawn fire engines. There is an 1815 hand-pumper and a 1907 three-horse Metropolitan steamer. The touches of brass and attention to detail on the fire equipment give it an artistic quality beyond its utilitarian value.

The museum's collection includes firemarks from old houses, helmets, badges, uniforms and a fireboat pilot house. A stained-glass window depicts rescue efforts by firefighters.

❺ Walk north on Second and turn right on Race Street. Here, ignored by most passersby on this short block in the shadow of the Benjamin Franklin Bridge, is another reminder of the past. Briefly stop at **136 Race (5)** to admire a 19th-century house with an unusual door carved to look like crepe (not open to the public). Philadelphia has many such details left over from its past—and many are waiting just around the corner.

❻ Now head south on Second, then turn east (left) on Arch Street toward the Delaware River to see a series of handsome 19th-century **iron-fronted buildings (6)** in the 100 block of Arch Street (not open to the public).

These structures were erected on the north side of the street in the mid-1800s and have been used commercially since then. They date from a time when Philadelphia was redefining itself. A center of intellect, religion, arts and letters, the city after the Civil War was becoming an industrial powerhouse, where business and technology flourished. By the time of the Centennial Exhibition in 1876, Philadelphia had entered what historians call its Iron Age—a time when the railroad was king, when factories and freight yards dotted the city and entrepreneur John Wanamaker loomed large with his successful department store and warehouses.

The mid-to-late 19th century saw widespread use of ornamental iron in architecture. One particularly fine example is at Eighth and Market Streets—the now-defunct Lit Brothers department store, which has been renovated and restored for use as retail space, offices and restaurants.

7 Retrace your steps and move west on Arch Street to one of Philadelphia's most popular tourist destinations, the **Betsy Ross House (7)** (*239 Arch Street*). This quaint brick townhouse is where Ross is said to have sewn the first American flag in 1777. (Open 10 a.m. to 5 p.m. Tuesday through Sunday, and on holiday Mondays. Free admission; donations accepted. Rest rooms available.)

Historians are not certain that Betsy Ross actually lived in the house. But if she didn't, she lived in one very similar, possibly a few doors away. Historians also are not sure that she sewed the first Stars and Stripes. But she did work for her family's flag and upholstery business, sewed pennants and ensigns for the state navy, and was well known for her skills as a seamstress.

Her fame, says historian Margaret Tinkcom, began to grow in 1870 when her grandson provided the Historical Society of Pennsylvania with an account given him as a child by the 84-year-old Ross herself. As the story goes, Betsy Ross said she had been asked to work on the flag by a committee that included George Washington, Robert Morris and George Ross. George Ross, a delegate to the Continental Congress, was the uncle of Betsy's husband, John Ross. John and Betsy Ross were involved in the patriot movement and joined the so-called Free Quakers, also known as "Fighting Quakers," who opposed British rule.

The Betsy Ross House was built about 1760 and is a fine example of an 18th-century Philadelphia house. It has a gabled roof, narrow, winding stairs, and eight rooms, including a basement kitchen, sitting room and bedrooms. Ross's reading glasses, chest of drawers and other period furniture recreate the atmosphere of the time.

Betsy Ross
House

Betsy was an industrious Quaker who outlived three husbands and died at 84. Following John Ross's death, she married Capt. Joseph Ashbourn on June 15, 1777, at Old Swedes' Church (Walk 5) as American colonists fought for independence. She is buried alongside her third husband, John Claypoole, in the brick-paved Atwater Kent Park, adjacent to the Betsy Ross House.

8 A walk further west on Arch Street takes you to the great iron gate of another historic landmark, **Loxley Court (8)** (*321 and 323 Arch Street*), a group of restored 18th-century houses where Benjamin Franklin is said to have flown the kite in his experiment with lightning.

One of the houses in this private, quiet court belonged to Benjamin Loxley, a carpenter who worked on Independence Hall and Carpenters' Hall. He was an early resident of the court and lived at Number 2. His front door key was said to be the one tied by Franklin to the kite during his experiment. Number 8 housed a tavern until the Methodists turned it into their second meeting house in 1768. They later moved to Old St. George's Church, 235 North Fourth Street, a site we will visit later in this tour. (Note: the residents of Loxley Court are fussy about keeping their iron gate closed. I closed it on my way out and was thanked by one of them.)

Next to Loxley Court is a firehouse and a garden adorned with a copper bust of Benjamin Franklin, cast from thousands of pennies collected for the 100th anniversary of Philadelphia's paid fire department.

9 Cross over to the south side of Arch to the **Arch Street Meeting House (9)** (*Fourth and Arch Streets*), a large, plain brick building constructed in 1804 for the Philadelphia Yearly Meeting of the Society of Friends. It is the oldest Quaker meeting house still in use in Philadelphia and the largest in the world. (Open 11 a.m. to 2 p.m. Monday to Friday from April through June; 1 to 4 p.m. Tuesday to Friday from June through November. Saturday 11 a.m. to 4 p.m. Admission is $2 per person. Closed to walk-in tours during the winter, but group tours can be scheduled. The site is still a center for worship and for a monthly meeting of Friends as well as the yearly meeting that focuses on administrative and business-related matters.)

Arch Street Meeting House

The meeting house was built on land given to the Quakers by William Penn in 1693. The ground was first used for burials, and many victims of the yellow fever epidemic of 1793 are interred here. The cry "Bring out your dead" was heard as carts bumped over the cobblestoned streets. The burials—including Samuel Nicholas, founder and first commandant of the United States Marine Corps—ended in 1803, and the meeting house was constructed the next year, following a design by Owen Biddle. The west wing was erected in 1811. Inside is a small museum with a slide show on William Penn and a series of dioramas depicting his life and contributions. Quaker artifacts also are exhibited, and there is a video on Quakerism.

10 Further west on Arch Street, beyond the Wyndham hotel, is the **Christ Church Burial Ground (10)** (*Fifth and Arch Streets*), the final resting place of five signers of the Declaration of Independence and many other colonial and Revolutionary War leaders who were celebrated in their time. But in this place of weathered headstones, the most famous occupant is Benjamin Franklin, who lies alongside his wife, Deborah. Their son, Francis, who died at age 4 in 1736, has a small marker. Visitors can walk through the cemetery from 10 a.m. to 4 p.m. Monday through Saturday, and noon to 4 p.m. on Sunday, weather permitting.

Benjamin Franklin's grave at Christ Church Burial Ground

About 20,000 people followed Franklin's body to its burial site in 1790. Thousands still come to see the grave each year—and many of them follow the local tradition of tossing a penny onto the grave for good luck. Franklin may have said, "A penny saved is a penny earned," but here people simply want to make a connection with him.

Franklin wrote an epitaph for himself in 1728, when he was 22 years old:

The Body
of
Benjamin Franklin
Printer
(Like the cover of an old book
Its contents torn out
And stript of its lettering and gilding)
Lies here, food for worms.
But the work shall not be lost
For it will (as he believed) appear once more
In a new and more elegant edition
Revised and corrected
by
The Author

In addition to Franklin, four other signers of the Declaration of Independence are buried here: Benjamin Rush, father of American psychiatry; Joseph Hewes, a Quaker merchant; George Ross, a delegate to the Continental Congress from New Jersey; and Francis Hopkinson, a composer and member of the Continental Congress from Philadelphia. Also buried here are Dr. John Kearsley, architect of Christ Church; Thomas Willing, president of the First Bank of the United States and a member of the Continental Congress; Philip Syng Physick, father of American surgery; Thomas Bond, a founder, with Benjamin Franklin, of the Pennsylvania Hospital; Capt. Richard Budden, who brought the Liberty Bell and the Christ Church bells from England; and John Dunlap, printer of the Declaration of Independence.

The burial ground was closed to the general public after the Bicentennial celebrations in 1976 because of the deteriorating condition of the tombs. It reopened to visitors free of charge in 2003 after hundreds of thousands of dollars in renovations had been completed.

⓫ Across from the burial ground is the **Free Quaker Meeting House (11)** (*500 Arch Street, on Independence Mall*), a restoration of the original 1783 building where a splinter group of "Fighting Quakers" worshipped. These Quakers took up arms against the British during the Revolutionary War. (New hours are forthcoming. In the past, it's been open Memorial Day to Labor Day, 10 a.m. to 4 p.m. Tuesday through Saturday, and Sunday from noon to 4 p.m.; other times of the year by appointment. Admission is free.)

The meeting house was designed by Samuel Wetherill and served as a place of worship until about 1834, when differences among the Quakers lessened. The members of the congregation included Betsy Ross, then Mrs. Claypoole. As the late local historian John Francis Marion once observed, Betsy was, "if anything, ecumenical before it was fashionable. We have seen her pew in Christ Church, and she was married to Joseph Ashbourn at Old Swedes'." Now, here she is, as Mrs. Claypoole, a Quaker in good standing at the Free Quaker Meeting House. Other congregants were Thomas Mifflin, a signer of the Constitution and a general in the Continental Army, and Clement Biddle, colonel in the Continental Army and quartermaster.

The Free Quakers eventually dissolved as a separate group, with many becoming Episcopalian. Their building was used as a school, library and warehouse. In the 1960s, restoration work began. The Free Quaker Meeting House was moved 33 feet west when Fifth Street was widened. Inside are two original benches and exhibits, including a five-pointed star pattern that Betsy Ross reportedly used to make the American flag. She could fold material in such a way as to make a five-pointed star with one snip.

Leaving the building, look at the inscription on a granite tablet in the north gable:

> By General Subscription
> For the Free Quakers, erected,
> In the year of our Lord, 1783,
> Of the Empire 8.

The last line is an apparent reference to the notion that the United States would become an empire, spreading its influence across the world.

⓬ Walk back across Fifth Street, then north across Arch to the **United States Mint (12)** (*Fifth and Arch Streets*), where visitors can see blank disks melted, cast and pressed into coins. The main entrance to the Mint is on Fifth Street. (General tour hours from 9 a.m. to 4:30 p.m. Monday through Friday, though closed on some federal holidays; in the summer season the Mint is open on Saturdays as well. Admission is free. No camera or video equipment is allowed.) The first Mint was constructed in 1792; this building was erected in 1971. Take the self-guided tour, walking along the gallery windows to see money made, inspected, counted and bagged. Or take a free guided tour, which lasts about 45 minutes. Also, stop in the lobby to see the Mint's mascot, Peter the Eagle. Guides used to tell children a fictitious story of how the eagle got his wing caught in a machine and wound up getting stuffed. The lobby also has a shop where you can buy coins and medals.

13 Leaving the Mint, turn left and walk south on Fifth Street past Christ Church Burial Ground to the **National Museum of American Jewish History (13)** (*Fifth Street and Market Street*), the only museum in the nation dedicated to documenting the Jewish experience in America. (Open 10 a.m. to 5 p.m. Tuesday through Friday; 10 a.m. to 5:30 p.m. Saturday and Sunday. Closed Monday but open on Martin Luther King Jr. Day, Presidents' Day, Independence Day and Christmas Day. Admission is $15 for adults; $13 for seniors and youth ages 13 to 21 or having college identification. Free for museum members, active-duty military and children 12 and under.)

Outside is a carrara marble statue depicting an allegorical figure of liberty protecting religious freedom. The work was commissioned by B'nai B'rith for the Centennial of the United States and dedicated in Fairmount Park on Thanksgiving, 1876. It was rededicated by B'nai B'rith International for the Bicentennial at this location. The statue of a female figure wears a liberty cap bordered by 13 stars, one for each of the original colonies. The youth at her feet represents religion. An American eagle crushes a serpent at the base, depicting the triumph of democracy over tyranny.

Through its programs and exhibitions of portraits and artifacts, the museum focuses on Jewish participation in the political, economic, social and cultural life of the nation. It has the largest collection of Jewish Americana in the world, with more than 30,000 objects.

14 Leave the museum, head east on Market Street, then north on Fourth Street for the home of **Congregation Mikveh Israel (14)** (*44 North Fourth Street*), which was established in 1740, making it the oldest Jewish congregation in Philadelphia and the second oldest in the nation. (To arrange a tour, call the synagogue, 215-922-5446. Open 9 a.m. to 5 p.m. Monday through Thursday; 9 a.m. to 3 p.m. on Friday; closed on Saturday and Sunday. Donations appreciated.)

The original synagogue was located at Third and Cherry Streets. Benjamin Franklin contributed to the building fund. Early members included Haym Salomon, a financier of the Revolution; Nathan Levy, a colonial merchant and one of the congregation's founding members; and Rebecca Gratz, who may have been the inspiration for the character Rebecca in Sir Walter Scott's novel *Ivanhoe*. According to a story told by Rebecca's nephew, Scott learned of her from author Washington Irving, one of Gratz's friends. Irving described her as a young, cultured and attractive Jewish woman who had been in love with a Christian but would not marry outside of her faith. She lived from 1781 to 1869 and devoted her life and financial resources to helping people. Gratz was one of the founders of the Female Association for the Relief of Women and Children in Reduced Circumstances, the Female Hebrew Benevolent Society and the Philadelphia Orphan Society. She also introduced portrait painter Thomas Sully to Philadelphia, helping launch his long career.

Artifacts here include George Washington's letter to the congregation. Mikveh Israel is one of four congregations in the world that uses the Sephardic, Spanish-Portuguese rite.

15 Leaving Mikveh Israel, walk to Fourth Street and head north. Passing under the Benjamin Franklin Bridge, you'll come to **St. George's United Methodist Church (15)** (*235 North Fourth Street*), the oldest continuously used Methodist church building in America. Called the "cradle of Methodism," St. George's has been in continuous use since 1769. (Open 10 a.m. to 4 p.m. Tuesday through Friday; Saturday morning by appointment. Free, though donations are encouraged. Services are held at 10 a.m. on Sunday. Phone 215-925-7788.)

The building was originally started about 1763 for a German Reformed congregation. They finished the roof and walls but ran out of funds. The simple brick structure was purchased by a local man and later sold to the Methodists, who moved in in 1769. Parishioners here listened to some of the best and most colorful preachers. British itinerant preacher Francis Asbury gave his first sermon in America here in 1771 and went on to become a leader of American Methodism. Another preacher, Thomas Webb, a military man, delivered sermons in his old uniform, with his sword lying across his

St. George's
United
Methodist
Church

Bible. He had come to America in 1755 as quartermaster under Gen. Edward Braddock and was seriously injured in the siege of Louisburg in 1775.

The church hosted conferences of American Methodism in 1773, 1774 and 1775. And it had ties to the Revolution. When Washington faced desperate times at Valley Forge in 1777, he turned to Robert Morris for the funds to feed and pay his starving army. Morris, a Philadelphia banker and merchant, spent a long night in prayer at St. George's before securing the funds. He was bankrupted by his efforts and was later jailed for failing to pay his debts. The British who occupied Philadelphia used the church for a cavalry school, since it still had a dirt floor and its front door opened on the street. The Methodist Historical Society adjoining the church has a large collection of memorabilia, including the Francis Asbury Bible, the John Wesley Chalice Cup, the Joseph Pilmoor Journal, and furniture and saddlebags used by circuit riders.

In the 1920s the church was almost destroyed. Planners of the Benjamin Franklin Bridge sought a right-of-way over the ground on which the church was built. But the courts ruled to save it by forcing relocation of the bridge, which was diverted 14 feet. The street had to be lowered, though, and the church is now several feet above it.

16 Opposite St. George's is another historic church, **Olde St. Augustine's Catholic Church (16)** (*243 North Lawrence Street*), a reconstruction of the church that was destroyed in anti-Catholic riots in 1844. (Open 9 a.m. to 5 p.m. Monday through Friday; 9 a.m. to the conclusion of evening masses on weekends. Free. Services: vigil, 5:15 p.m. on Saturday; mass 9 a.m., 11 a.m. and 7 p.m. on Sunday; 12:05 p.m. on weekdays; legal holidays at 10 a.m.)

The parish was established in 1796, and the original church was erected in 1798. It was destroyed on May 8, 1844, by anti-Catholic mobs. The violence was set off by a letter written by Bishop Kenrick on November 14, 1842, to the board of controllers of public schools,

Olde St. Augustine's Catholic Church

requesting that Catholic children be permitted to use their own Bible and be excused from other religious instruction in the public schools. Anti-Catholic groups used the request to launch a kind of holy war.

After its destruction in the riots, St. Augustine's was rebuilt in 1847. (The church's architect, Napoleon Le Brun, also designed the Academy of Music and the Cathedral of SS. Peter and Paul. Both will be visited on upcoming walks.) The church was consecrated in 1848 by the Irish friars of the Order of St. Augustine. From this site, Augustinians carried their missionary work into New England, the Hudson Valley, South Jersey and Philadelphia's Main Line. St. Augustine's Academy was founded here in 1811 and was the forerunner of Villanova University.

St. Augustine's and St. George's were examples of Penn's dream, set down in his 1701 Charter of Privileges for Pennsylvanians. He wrote that "noe people can be truly happy though under the Great Enjoyments of Civil Liberties if Abridged of the Freedom of theire Consciences as to theire Religious Profession and Worship."

17 Looming overhead is another Philadelphia landmark, the **Benjamin Franklin Bridge (17)** (*Fifth and Vine Streets*). At almost two miles, it was the longest suspension bridge in the world when it opened in 1926. The Ben Franklin is highly recommended to bridge-walkers for the magnificent views of the city from its deck. (A pedestrian walkway is open 6 a.m. to 8 p.m. daily from October 1 to April 30, and 6 a.m. to 9 p.m. from May 1 to September 30. Free. Pedestrians are not allowed on the Walt Whitman Bridge further south.)

The main suspension cables, 30 inches in diameter, and the smaller vertical cables that hold the road deck, create the impression of a spider's web. From the pedestrian walkway, cars, trucks and trains speed by below you and ships glide 150 feet below on the river.

18 At the Philadelphia end of the bridge, pause to look at the "Bolt of Lightning" sculpture, which celebrates Franklin's lightning experiment. Then walk west on Race Street to **Franklin Square (18)** (*Sixth and Race Streets*), one of William Penn's five original squares.

The trees and grass in this park once were surrounded by houses and churches. Poet Walt Whitman was among the more famous bench-warmers here. Although the buildings have been replaced

Benjamin
Franklin Bridge

by rushing traffic, the lovely green oasis and the benches remain, reminders of a less hurried time. Take a break. Enjoy the fountain, which in season features choreographed shows of dancing water, lights and music.

19 Leaving the square, cross Race Street and walk south on Seventh Street to the **African American Museum in Philadelphia (19)** (*701 Arch Street*), the first museum specifically funded and built in a major American city to house and interpret artifacts, fine art, crafts and culture of African Americans. (Open 10 a.m. to 5 p.m. Wednesday through Saturday, noon to 5 p.m. on Sunday. Adults $14; children 4 to 12, students with ID and seniors $10. Open on Dr. Martin Luther King Jr. Day.)

The museum was founded during the Bicentennial year of 1976

and has helped showcase black intellectual and artistic activities, with a focus on Philadelphia and Pennsylvania. A permanent exhibit—"Audacious Freedom—African Americans in Philadelphia 1776–1876"—recounts the stories and contributions by people of African descent during the years following the birth of the nation. The gift shop is a must for those interested in books on black history, culture, fiction, drama and poetry. The shop also has African sculpture and textiles, as well as prints and jewelry.

20 About five blocks north of the museum on Seventh Street is the **Edgar Allan Poe National Historic Site (20)** (*532 North Seventh Street at Spring Garden Street*), where the famous writer and poet lived from 1842 to 1844, penning some of his best-known short stories. Not far from Old City, the site can be reached on the SEPTA

Edgar Allan Poe National Historic Site

Route 47 bus, which runs along Seventh Street to Spring Garden. (Open 9 a.m. to noon and 1 p.m. to 5 p.m. Friday through Sunday.)

A statue of a sinister-looking bird will catch the eye as you approach Poe's house; it commemorates one of his greatest works, "The Raven." Beyond it is the 19th-century, three-story brick house that was home to Poe; his wife (and cousin), Virginia; his mother-in-law, Maria Clemm; and their cat. Several of Poe's most famous short stories were published while he lived here, among them "The Black Cat," "The Tell-Tale Heart" and "The Gold Bug." Poe moved a lot during his brief life, making stops along the way in Philadelphia, then the hub of the American publishing world. But his goals seemed to always elude him. He dreamed of issuing his own magazine and eventually bought a New York periodical, only to watch it fail for lack of capital. Poe sometimes drank excessively. In 1849, he was found in a drunken stupor in a Baltimore gutter and soon died. He was 40 years old.

For Poe fans and history buffs alike, a tour of his small house is well worth the trip. Imagine the writer within these walls, the chilling stories put on paper here. If you can't quite conjure it, a brief film and other exhibits will help. The Poe house offers a delightful end to our walk.

Society Hill

Society Hill

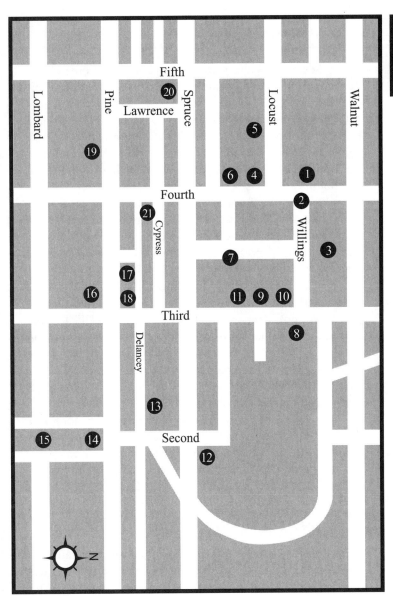

WALK 3

USEFUL INFORMATION

The Society Hill and waterfront areas have scores of restaurants and dining establishments, among them La Famiglia Ristorante, 8 South Front Street; South Street Diner, 140 South Street; the Olde Bar in the landmark Old Original Bookbinder's site, 125 Walnut Street; Marrakesh, 517 South Leithgow Street; and Moshulu, the world's oldest and largest four-masted sailing ship, moored on the Delaware River at 401 South Columbus Boulevard, Penn's Landing.

Parking for the Society Hill walk is available on Second Street between Chestnut and Walnut Streets, at Second and Lombard Streets, and at Third and Lombard Streets. Numerous metered parking spaces also are available throughout the area. For visitors to nearby Penn's Landing (Walk 4), parking lots can be accessed from Columbus Boulevard (Delaware Avenue), which runs along the waterfront.

If you're not driving, the city's transit system (SEPTA) runs through the area (see the Useful Information section in Walk 1 for details). At your disposal are buses, subway cars, trains and trolley service, including the PHLASH, the colorful, purple shuttle. The PHLASH's downtown bus loop stops at the major tourist districts day and night.

Once you're there, horse-drawn carriages or motorized, Victorian-style trolleys also are available. Carriages may be hired on Independence Mall and trolleys can be boarded at the Independence Visitors Center, 5th and Market Streets.

Introduction

The name comes from a commercial venture that failed more than 300 years ago—and from a characteristic of the land that has virtually disappeared with time. But say "Society Hill" today, and many people don't think of business or geography. They think of charming colonial and Federal-style brick rowhouses, lavish mansions and handsome courtyards. They think of cobblestoned streets, picturesque corners, small private gardens and horse-drawn carriages. Those images of a bygone time are part of Philadelphia's most photogenic residential community.

The "society" in the area's name refers to the Free Society of Traders, a short-lived, 17th-century British corporation that invested in William Penn's new colony and was given a strip of land that included a hill at the foot of Pine Street near the Delaware River. More than 200 subscribers put money into the enterprise and apparently anticipated great success. A 1682 prospectus indicated that the Free Society of Traders was expecting no less than a takeover of the maritime commerce through its trading stations at Philadelphia and on the Chesapeake Bay. In the following year, the corporation's holdings included a tannery, a sawmill and a glasshouse. But the Pennsylvania Assembly didn't support monopolies and did not confirm the company's charter. By 1686, the Society was headed for bankruptcy and abandoned its trading operations. And by 1723, its last holdings had been dispersed.

In the years that followed, the hill that was part of the Society's land grant eroded and was nearly leveled. But the name of the place lived on over the centuries, the last vestige of an abortive business enterprise.

The people who moved into the community tended to be well-to-do and more open about dancing, music and theater than the more conservative Quakers who settled further north in Old City. Yet Society Hill folks also focused on religious matters—as they did in 1739 and 1740, when thousands came to hear George Whitefield, the eloquent Calvinist Methodist preacher and apostle of the "Great Awakening" in the middle and southern colonies. Huge crowds gathered around him, hanging on every word as he gave passionate sermons from a stage.

A friend of Whitefield's, Benjamin Franklin, described the preacher's sermons with admiration. "He had a loud and clear voice, and articulated his words and sentences so perfectly, that he might be heard and understood at a great distance, especially as his auditories, however numerous, observ'd the most exact silence," wrote Franklin in his autobiography. "By hearing him often, I came to distinguish easily between sermons newly compos'd, and those which he had often preach'd in the course of his travels. His delivery of the latter was so improv'd by frequent repetitions that every accent, every emphasis, every modulation of voice, was so perfectly well turn'd and well plac'd, that, without being interested in the subject, one could not help being pleas'd with the discourse; a pleasure of much the same kind with that receiv'd from an excellent piece of musick."

More houses went up in Society Hill during the 19th century as the area became increasingly residential. Many of those houses remain today—not as a collection of museums or historic sites but as a neighborhood of homes. The community prospered over the years, generally spreading from the Delaware River west to Sixth Street and from Walnut south to Lombard Street.

But Society Hill fell on hard times after World War I, with many houses becoming rundown and historic mansions becoming tenements. Waves of immigrants and poor blacks from the rural South moved into the crowded rowhouses. Rebirth and renewal came in the 1950s, thanks to the efforts of the Philadelphia Redevelopment Authority, the City Historical Commission, the City Planning Commission and other federal, civic and private agencies. Historically significant properties were identified and purchased by the city, which then resold them to people who would restore them. Among the sites refurbished and rebuilt was Head House Square, an open-air colonial marketplace.

The transformation of Society Hill helped spark changes across the city, and it became a model for other urban areas trying to restore and rebuild. Today, this vibrant community is filled with notable churches and magnificent mansions, all returned to their former glory. Indeed, the image of Society Hill comes to mind whenever people think of Philadelphia.

The Tour

❶ Begin your walk on the south side of Independence Square, at Fifth and Walnut Streets (visited in Walk 1). Head east on Walnut to Fourth Street, turn right and continue on the west side of Fourth to the **Philadelphia Contributionship for the Insurance of Houses from Loss by Fire (1)** (*212 South Fourth Street*), the head office of the oldest fire insurance company in the United States. (Open weekdays, 8:30 a.m. to 5 p.m. Free admission.)

The company that occupied this elegant Greek Revival house, with fluted Corinthian columns of marble and magnificent salons, was founded by Benjamin Franklin and his friends in 1752. Franklin helped establish a fire-fighting system in which insurance companies were responsible for battling blazes, as well as paying for losses. Earlier, fires were fought by volunteers with little more than buckets and ladders.

The Contributionship's building was designed by Thomas Ustick Walter and was erected in 1836. Sign the guest book on the first floor and tour a small museum that contains a collection of firemen's hats, a small fire engine, lanterns and firemarks. The firemark of the Contributionship was the hand-in-hand, designed by silversmith Philip Syng, a director of the company.

Next, head to the second floor and take a peek into a rich-looking boardroom with crystal chandeliers and mahogany cane-seated chairs. A seating plan on the wall shows Benjamin Franklin as the first incumbent of seat No. 1.

2 Across the street from the fire insurance company is historic **Willing's Alley (2)** (*off the 200 block of Fourth Street near the intersection with Walnut Street*), a narrow, 18th-century cobblestoned street. It is named for Thomas Willing, a pre–Revolutionary War mayor of the city and a partner of banker Robert Morris, who helped finance the Revolution.

3 Willing's Alley leads to our next stop, **Old St. Joseph's Church (3)** (*321 Willing's Alley*), established in 1733 as the first Roman Catholic Church in Philadelphia. (Rectory hours, 9:30 a.m. to 4 p.m.

Old St. Joseph's Church

Monday to Friday; 9 a.m. to 2 p.m. on Sunday. Masses at 12:05 p.m. Monday to Saturday; vigil mass at 5:30 p.m. on Saturday; Sunday masses at 7:30, 9:30 and 11:30 a.m. and 6:30 p.m.)

Beyond the archway, with its iron gates, is an inner courtyard leading to the rectory on the right, and beyond it, the church. The original church was built here in 1733 and hidden from view by surrounding buildings—for a reason. Catholic worship was prohibited in England, and though religious freedom was promised in Pennsylvania, parishioners here had to be security-conscious. The church was enlarged in 1821 and later rebuilt. The present structure dates to 1838.

St. Joseph's survived the anti-Catholic riots of 1844, when some churches were burned. The sanctuary is impressive, with its 19th-century stained-glass windows and painting of the crucifixion behind the altar. Among those attending mass here on at least one occasion were George Washington, John Adams and the Marquis de Lafayette. Commodore John Barry, known as the father of the United States Navy, was a parishioner.

❹ Leaving Old St. Joseph's, return to Fourth Street and walk south to the **Shippen-Wistar House (4)** (*Fourth and Locust Streets*), a colonial-era home that once belonged to wealthy Philadelphia physicians and is privately owned. (Not open to the public.)

This well-proportioned brick house was built in 1750 and first occupied by its builder, William Shippen Sr., prominent doctor and delegate to the Continental Congress. It was later the home of his physician son, Dr. William Shippen Jr., a professor of anatomy and surgery at the College of Philadelphia (now the University of Pennsylvania) and director general of the Medical Service of the Continental Army. As a teacher, he was among the first to use human bodies for dissection in his classes and became a controversial figure because of his "body-snatching" activities.

The house was sold in 1798 to Casper Wistar, a physician at the Pennsylvania Hospital and a professor of anatomy at the University of Pennsylvania. Wistar was a member of the American Philosophical Society and succeeded Thomas Jefferson as its president. He held parties at the house for members of Philadelphia society and for visiting scholars, statesmen and scientists. What conversations must have taken place within these walls!

Before moving on, notice the decorative iron fence to the rear of the house and the lovely garden and fountain. Many private gardens and small public parks are hidden away amid the neat, ruddy brick rowhouses of Society Hill, making it one of the most pleasant of places to take a walk.

5 Take a few more steps west on Locust Street and you're at the entrance to the **Magnolia Tribute Garden (5)** (*south side of Locust between Fourth and Fifth Streets*). The garden is a peaceful place, with a fountain and benches. It was created and has been maintained by the Garden Club of America in honor of the nation's founders. George Washington was especially fond of horticulture and would have enjoyed this beautiful setting.

6 Return to Fourth Street and walk south (a right turn) to **Old St. Mary's Church (6)** (*252 South Fourth Street*), the first cathedral of the Diocese of Philadelphia and the city's main Catholic church during the Revolutionary War period. (Mass schedule: chapel 7:30 a.m. daily; Saturday vigil 4:30 p.m.; Sunday mass at 10 a.m.)

Founded in 1763, Old St. Mary's is the second-oldest Catholic Church in the city. It was enlarged in 1810, received a Gothic-style facade in 1880 and was renovated in 1963 and again in 1979. The ornamental interior, high altar and crucifixion window are noteworthy. Washington attended services here, as he did at other churches in the city.

Many prominent people are buried in the small churchyard, among them Commodore John Barry, the Revolutionary War naval hero; Thomas FitzSimons, a signer of the Constitution; Stephen Moylan, aide-de-camp to Washington; Michael Bouvier, great-great-grandfather of Jacqueline Kennedy Onassis; Matthew Carey, a leading Philadelphia printer and publisher; and George Meade, grandfather of Gen. George Gordon Meade, hero of the Battle of Gettysburg in the Civil War.

7 Walk back to Locust Street, cross Fourth Street, then duck through a break in the houses into a contemporary courtyard, **Bingham Court (7)** (*200 block of South Fourth Street*), a charming, tree-shaded setting amid brown brick homes. One of Philadelphia's delights is the presence of quiet courtyards, open-air oases in the heart of the city. Whether tiny colonial gardens or modern courtyards like this one, these parks and walkways soften the harshness of the urban environment. Philadelphia is like London in that respect.

8 Return to the adjacent Willing's Alley and make your way east toward **Old St. Paul's Church (8)** (*225 South Third Street*), the third Episcopal church in the city when it was built in 1761. It is now the headquarters of the Episcopal Community Services of Philadelphia. (Churchyard open from 9 a.m. to about 5 p.m. Monday through Friday.)

The Greek Revival building, designed by William Strickland, was converted to a hospital during the British occupation of Philadelphia and filled with the casualties of both armies after the Battle of Germantown. The dead were buried in mass graves without coffins. Others buried here in marked graves include Gen. Thomas Proctor, who fought in the Whiskey Rebellion, and Edwin Forrest, the renowned tragedian whose feud with the English actor William Macready caused the Astor Place Riot in New York in 1849. Thirty people were killed during a demonstration by Forrest partisans against Macready.

9 Leaving Old St. Paul's, head south on Third Street to **Powel House (9)** (*244 South Third Street*), an elegant Georgian townhouse that once belonged to Samuel Powel, the last colonial mayor of Philadelphia and first mayor after the Revolution. (Open 11 a.m. to 3 p.m. Thursday through Saturday, from April to November; 12 to 3 p.m. on Sunday. Weekends only in March and December; closed in the last two weekends of December. January and February by appointment only. Call 215-627-0364. Admission $8; $6 for students and seniors, and $20 per family.) The site is owned and managed by the Philadelphia Society for the Preservation of Landmarks.

The stately brick house with white trim was erected by Charles Stedman in 1765 and purchased by Powel in 1768. Inside, Powel made it a place of great beauty, with paneled pine walls painted in soft colors, bas-relief plastered ceilings and mahogany wainscoting. The property includes a formal garden, one of the loveliest in Society Hill. Many of the colonial period's most famous people dined here.

Powel died of yellow fever during the outbreak in 1793. His house, scheduled for razing in 1930, was saved, then restored to its former glory. The lavish interior is set off by 18th-century art, a gilt-framed mirror, oil paintings, period furniture, exquisite porcelain, silver and a staircase of Santo Domingo mahogany. One of the most-prized possessions is a signed Gilbert Stuart portrait of Anne Pennington.

Strolling through this imposing house is truly stepping back in time. Imagine the parties held here by Powel's wife, Elizabeth. And

Powel House

picture the distinguished guests roaming the halls, dancing in the second-floor ballroom or standing off in a corner, talking about the nation's future.

10 Next door to the Powel House stands the home of **John Penn (10)** (*242 South Third Street*), grandson of William Penn and the last colonial governor of Pennsylvania. (Not open to the public.)

John Penn took up his duties as governor in 1763, at the end of the French and Indian War, and found enormous challenges. The proprietorship of such a huge area would be daunting. Penn found the collection of rents difficult and watched the peaceful relationship with Native Americans deteriorate as westward-moving settlers clashed with tribes on the frontier. Penn's problems grew worse as the rift between America and England grew wider. John Penn and his uncle, Thomas Penn, referred to that split as "the Storm gathering." When the Second Continental Congress met in Philadelphia in the summer of 1775, John Penn wrote, "Our form of government still continues but I think it cannot last long." He was right. The colonies declared independence in 1776, and Pennsylvania rewrote its constitution. John Penn was forced into exile and eventually retired to his country house to wait out the war.

Another famous owner of the Penn house was Benjamin Chew, the last colonial chief justice of Pennsylvania. The home was later the residence of Juan de Miralles, the first Spanish diplomatic representative to the United States, and his successor, Francisco Rondon.

① The houses from **258 to 262 on the west side of Third Street (11)** are brownstones built in 1849 and were owned by Michael Bouvier, great-great-grandfather of Jacqueline (Bouvier) Kennedy Onassis. Bouvier, who made his living as a cabinet maker and mahogany merchant, came to this country from France after the French Revolution. He is buried in St. Mary's Cemetery.

⑫ Walk south on Third to Spruce Street, turn left and head east about a block to our next stop: **Man Full of Trouble Tavern (12)** *(125–127 Spruce Street)*, a restoration of the oldest tavern remaining from colonial Philadelphia. It has been maintained as a museum by the Knauer Foundation.

The red brick tavern and the adjacent Paschall House were erected about 1759 on the banks of Little Dock Creek and were probably the closest buildings to the Delaware River. The creek has been filled in, and changes in the area have put more distance between these buildings and the river. But a sense of history still clings to the structures, which sit in the shadow of Society Hill Towers, three high-rise apartment towers that have been controversial since they were built in the early 1960s. The 31-story buildings, which contrast sharply in scale with the two- and three-story townhouses around them, were designed by I. M. Pei and put up after a slum clearance of the old Dock Street market site. It is hard to imagine more incongruous buildings in the heart of a historic district.

Col. Blaithwaite Jones, commander of the river defenses against the British forces, was one of the early owners of the Man Full of Trouble Tavern. Musket slots can be seen on the landings between the first and second floor and were to be used to fend off an attack. But this colorful place had more social significance than military. Here is a piece of the city's nautical past. Many seafarers patronized the tavern, which was licensed to provide lodgings and serve food

Man Full of Trouble Tavern

and drink. Its attic quarters were small, with low ceilings like the cabins of an 18th-century ship, but they must have seemed down-right luxurious to sailors after months at sea.

The tavern's name is Biblical, from Job 14:1: "Man that is born of a woman is of few days, and full of trouble."

We are now a block from the Delaware River and adjacent to Inter-state 95. Several parks and footbridges traverse the highway, leading to Penn's Landing and the waterfront. At Spruce Street an area of decking over the interstate contains the Philadelphia Vietnam Veter-ans Memorial. We'll come back to this area on Walk 4.

Cross cobblestoned Spruce Street, walk south on Second to De-lancey Street and turn right. This tree-shaded street, one of the love-liest in Society Hill, makes for a delightful stroll.

13 Continue west to the **Rhoads-Barclay House (13)** (*217 Delancey Street at Philip Street*), a two-and-a-half-story colonial town-house built by Samuel Rhoads in 1758 for Alexander Barclay, comp-troller of the Port of Philadelphia. (Not open to the public.)

Rhoads was a member of the Carpenters' Company and built Benjamin Franklin's house, as well as much of Pennsylvania Hospital. He also was a delegate to the First Continental Congress and a mayor of Philadelphia. The house later was connected to a colonial-style structure erected next door and became part of a single private home.

Now take in the rest of the block—the historic red brick houses, the flags fluttering in the breeze, tiny alleys and small gardens. Take a peek at Drinker's Court on the south side of the 200 block of Delancey. And read the signs in the windows of several historic houses giving the date of construction in the 1700s and the name of the owner and his occupation.

The house at 222 Delancey was built in 1843 for Jacob Weaver and Henry Valkomar, "grate and stove manufacturers." The house at 244 Delancey was built in 1766 and belonged to Norton Pryor, "gentleman." Other details on the block are charming—the black iron fence around a garden at Philip and Delancey Streets, the wavy imperfections in the glass of some windowpanes and the metal boot scraper outside No. 232, used to clean mud off footwear before entering the house.

Wander into the 300 block of Delancey. The Federal-style house at No. 306 once belonged to Benjamin Worrel, a house carpenter. A little further along the brick sidewalk, you'll come to a small, tree-shaded park with benches and a playground for children.

14–**15** Return now to Second Street and head south toward **Head House (14)** (*Second and Pine Streets*), a handsome, brick Georgian structure built in 1803 as the office and residence of the market master, who collected fees and checked the quality of goods in the adjacent marketplace.

The landmark structure dominates **Head House Square (15)** (*Second Street from Pine to Lombard Streets*), an open-air brick arcade that served as a colonial market and is now flanked on both sides by charming shops and restaurants. (Open and free.)

An island amid the traffic flow on cobblestoned Second Street, these arcades remind us of the way people used to buy their daily produce. The market was built in 1745 and continued to have a few stalls as late as the 1950s. The site was restored in the 1960s. It is now a delightful place to visit, especially in summer, when it bustles with crafts people, artists and entertainers.

Head House Square

⓰ From Head House Square, walk west on Pine Street one block to **St. Peter's Church (16)** (*313 Pine Street*), one of the oldest and most beautiful colonial churches in the city. (Open to public 8 a.m. to 4 p.m. Monday through Friday; 8 a.m. to 1 p.m. Saturday; and 9 a.m. to 3 p.m. Sunday. Guided tours 11 a.m. to 1 p.m. on Saturday and 1 to 3 p.m. on Sunday. Worship services at 9 a.m. and 11 a.m. on Sunday).

A Society Hill landmark, St. Peter's has been in use since 1761. The church was founded by members of Christ Church who had settled in the Society Hill area. Episcopal Bishop William White, the rector of Christ Church, also served as rector of St. Peter's. This handsome brick church was designed by Scottish architect Robert Smith and built between 1761 and 1763. The plain steeple was designed by William Strickland and was added to the top of the tall, slim belfry in 1842. Inside, the overall layout, wine-glass pulpit, ornate organ case

Steeple of St. Peter's Church *(seen from cemetery next to Old Pine Street Church)*

and original pews remain, including No. 41, where the Washingtons sat with Samuel and Elizabeth Powel, whom we met earlier on stop No. 9.

In the churchyard, overshadowed by giant sycamores and elms, are the graves of a number of famous Americans. Among them: naval hero Stephen Decatur, who was killed in a duel by longtime enemy Commodore James Barron; Benjamin Chew, chief justice of Pennsylvania and owner of Cliveden, a Georgian manor house in Germantown; Dr. William Shippen, the prominent physician and delegate to the Continental Congress; Nicholas Biddle, diplomat and financier; Charles Willson Peale, the great portrait painter; and seven Native American chiefs who died of smallpox during a visit to the city in 1793.

17 Across Pine Street from the church is **St. Peter's Way (17)** (*300 block of Pine Street*), a pleasant greenwalk leading to Delancey Street and a playground-park for children. Follow a red brick pathway and enter this verdant oasis. Here's a quiet spot to take a break on a bench amid historic houses and old-style lamp posts. The park was dedicated in 1966 in memory of Rev. William De Lancey, rector of St. Peter's parish and provost of the University of Pennsylvania.

18 In the same block of Pine Street, on the northwest corner of Pine and Third, is the **Thaddeus Kosciuszko National Memorial (18)** (*301 Pine Street*). This was the home of the Polish general, statesman and patriot who distinguished himself during the American Revolution. (Open 12 to 4 p.m. April through October; closed November through March.)

Kosciuszko came to America in 1776 and was one of the first foreign volunteers to fight under George Washington. An engineer trained in the art of military fortification, he designed defenses at Philadelphia, West Point and Saratoga during the Revolution. His work at Saratoga led to the American victory in 1777 and helped encourage France to enter the war as America's ally. Kosciuszko, said Thomas Jefferson, was "as pure a son of liberty as I have ever known, and of that liberty which is to go to all, and not to the few or the rich alone."

The Polish soldier left America for his homeland in 1793 to lead an unsuccessful uprising against the Russian czar. Kosciuszko was captured, imprisoned and later freed by the czar. He returned to the United States and lived in the plain, three-story Georgian brick boarding house at 301 Pine Street during the winter of 1797–98. But he left again for Poland in 1798, was again defeated and retired to Switzerland, where he later died.

19 Society Hill is blessed with historic churches, and we're about to visit another one. Walk west on Pine and cross Fourth Street to **Old Pine Street Church (19)** (*412 Pine Street*), the only Presbyterian house of worship remaining in Philadelphia from colonial times. Its parishioners' strong support of the Revolution earned it the title "Church of the Patriots." (Open to public 8:30 a.m. to 4:30 p.m. Monday through Friday. Services at 10:30 a.m. on Sunday. Guided tours available by appointment.)

Known affectionately by local residents as "Old Pine," the building was designed by architect Robert Smith and erected by James Armitage, a member of the Carpenters' Company, between 1766 and

Old Pine Street Church

1768. It sits on land granted by Thomas and Richard Penn in 1764 "for the use of Presbyterians forever."

The church's pastor, George Duffield, was an ardent patriot and served as chaplain to the First Continental Congress and to the Pennsylvania Militia. Sixty-five members of the congregation served in the Revolutionary Army, 35 of them as officers. But the church's stand carried a price. The building was damaged by occupying British forces, who used it as a military hospital and a stable and burned the pews as firewood. About 100 Hessians are buried in the churchyard along the east wall of the church.

In more peaceful times, "Old Pine" drew many famous visitors, including John Adams, Dr. William Shippen and Benjamin Rush, the American physician who urged Thomas Paine to write "Common Sense."

The church, which through mergers also became known as the Third, Scots, and Mariners Presbyterian Church, was remodeled between 1837 and 1857 and transformed from Georgian to Greek Revival. The roof was raised, and Corinthian columns were paired across the front like a classic temple's.

The adjacent churchyard contains more than 3,000 graves. They include the burial sites of William Hurry, who is said to have rung the Liberty Bell at the first public reading of the Declaration of Independence; Col. William Linnard, who positioned cannon at the mouth of Wissahickon Creek and fired on the Hessians at the Battle of Germantown; Gen. John Steele, a parishioner who served as Washington's aide-de-camp and was present at Yorktown when the British surrendered; and the church's sixth pastor, Thomas Brainerd, an anti-slavery leader in the city.

20 Across from Old Pine Street Church, enter Lawrence Street, a small, north-south artery, and follow it to Lawrence Court. Proceed to the **Society Hill Synagogue (20)** (*418 Spruce Street*), a fascinating Greek Revival structure erected in 1829 as the Spruce Street Baptist Church. (Kabbalat Shabbat service at 6:15 p.m. on Friday. Shabbat service at 10 a.m. on Saturday. B'nai Mitzvah service at 9:30 a.m. Visitors welcome at other times. For tours, call for appointment, 215-922-6590.)

The massive, ornate building was designed by architect Thomas Ustick Walter, before he left the city in 1851 to work on the dome and the House and Senate wings of the Capitol in Washington. Walter was a Philadelphia native and a prominent Baptist who was responsible for many buildings here. This Spruce Street site was a church until 1909, when it became the home of the Rumanian-American

Society Hill Synagogue

Congregation Oir Chodosh Agudas-Achim. It was taken over in 1967 by a Conservative congregation and became the Society Hill Synagogue. The building has been through four major interior and exterior renovations since 1967.

㉑ Return to Lawrence Court, turn left on Cypress Street and follow it across Fourth Street to the **Hill-Physick-Keith House (21)** (*321 South Fourth Street at Delancey Street*). This is the only freestanding house in Society Hill and is one of the most splendid residences in America from the Federal period. (Open 11 a.m. to 3 p.m. Thursday through Saturday, from April to November; 11 a.m. to 3 p.m. Wednesdays from Memorial Day to Labor Day; weekends only in March and December; closed the last two weekends of December; January and February by appointment only. Call 215-925-7866 to schedule. Admission $8; seniors and students $6 and families $20.)

This elegant brick house was built in 1786 by merchant Henry Hill, who lived here until his death four years later. The house was

Hill-Physick-Keith House

Hill-Physick-Keith House

bought by Abigail Physick, who later gave it to her brother, the most famous occupant, Dr. Philip Syng Physick, who is known as the "father of American surgery." The physician lived here from 1815 until his death in 1837, when the house passed through various descendants to Mrs. Charles Penrose Keith. It was restored in 1965 with money from the Annenberg Fund and is managed by the Philadelphia Society for the Preservation of Landmarks.

Notice the well-proportioned exterior and the large fanlight in the entrance hall. And feel the spaciousness of the rooms, filled with magnificent Federal and Empire furniture from the time Dr. Physick lived here. Also on display are venerable oil paintings and silver. One meeting room is devoted to the Society of the Cincinnati, descendants of high-ranking Revolutionary War officers who served with George Washington. The group is named after the legendary Roman citizen-soldier Cincinnatus, who left his small farm to lead an army, then returned to it after victory. Washington was on hand at the founding of the society in Fishkill, New York, in 1783; its purpose was to preserve what the officers had fought for and to promote the "dignity of the American empire." A game table once used by Washington is one of the treasures in this room.

Before leaving the Hill-Physick-Keith House and ending Walk 3, visit the sprawling gardens, considered among the loveliest in Philadelphia. They are planted on three sides of the house and include plants common to 19th-century gardens. Stroll along the winding path past Pompeiian statues. The Roman city of Pompeii, buried under volcanic ash when Mt. Vesuvius erupted in 79 A.D., had just been excavated at the time of the house's construction, and related items were popular. You'll also see a natural grotto and antique cannon.

The visit makes for a pleasant end to our tour of Society Hill.

Penn's Landing

Penn's Landing

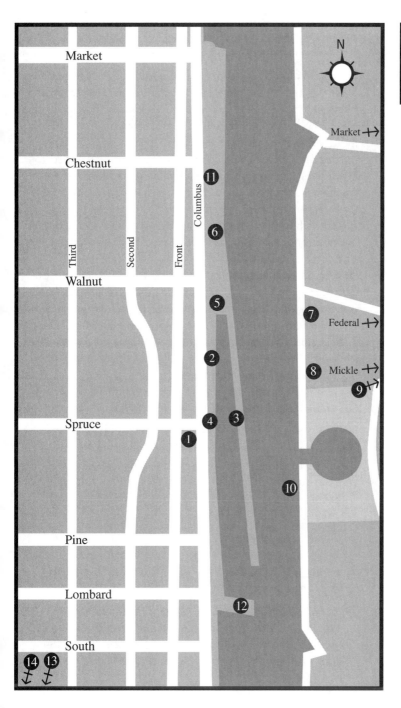

N

Market

Chestnut

Columbus

Walnut

Third

Second

Front

Market →→

11

6

5

Federal →→

7

2

8

Mickle →→

9 →→

4

3

Spruce

1

10

Pine

Lombard

12

South

14 13

USEFUL INFORMATION

Dining experiences here can be unique. Consider a meal on the beautifully restored *Moshulu*, the world's oldest and largest four-masted sailing ship, docked on the Delaware River, 401 South Columbus Boulevard. (Dinner 5 p.m. to 10 p.m. Monday through Sunday; brunch 11 a.m. to 2:30 p.m. on Saturday and 10 a.m. to 2:30 p.m. on Sunday. Call ahead for reservations, 215-923-2500.) Or if you'd like a cruise and musical entertainment with your lunch or dinner, try one of the cruise vessels docked at Penn's Landing (see below). Other restaurants here include the Chart House, 555 South Columbus Boulevard at Penn's Landing, and South Street Diner, 140 South Street.

Public parking lots can be accessed from Columbus Boulevard (Delaware Avenue), which runs along the waterfront. Metered parking also is available throughout the area. For getting around, the PHLASH, the colorful, purple shuttle bus, can be useful. The shuttle makes loops from the waterfront and South Street through Center City to Logan Circle, stopping at historic sites and attractions.

Cruise vessels also are available along Penn's Landing, including these:

- *The Spirit of Philadelphia (401 S. Columbus Boulevard)* is a sleek-looking, largely enclosed vessel offering lunch and dinner trips with a buffet spread, live floor show and dancing. Two- to three-hour lunch and dinner cruises available. (For reservations and current prices, call 866-455-3866.)

- *Ben Franklin Yacht (101 S. Columbus Boulevard)* offers a live DJ with a full range of music and a 60" flat screen TV for presentations or sports. (For information on reservations and prices, call 215-351-5333.)

- *Freedom Elite Yacht (401 S. Columbus Boulevard)* provides a house sound system/satellite radio and can make a DJ available for an additional fee. (Call 215-923-2469.)

Introduction

Illiam Penn headed up the Delaware River in the fall of 1682
to a sparsely populated frontier community that was short
on amenities but blessed with great potential. Penn's ship, the *Welcome*, passed lush forests laced with streams and anchored in a deep, commodious harbor. And from this place, now aptly called Penn's Landing, he began building the "Greene Country Towne" he called Philadelphia.

The new town had only a few hundred inhabitants in 1683 but grew quickly. One of the largest investors in the area, Robert Turner, built the first brick house at Front and Mulberry Streets in 1684. The following year, Turner wrote to Penn in England: "The Town of Philadelphia it goeth on in Planting and Building to admiration . . . many brave Brick Houses are going up."

By 1700, Philadelphia had more than 300 houses and at least 2,000 residents. And over the decades that followed, its riverfront became increasingly busy with tall-masted sailing ships carrying more people and cargo to the "City of Brotherly Love." Sturdy buildings rose everywhere and church spires pierced the sky as Penn's city grew westward toward the Schuylkill.

Private Johann Conrad Dohla, one of 30,000 Hessian mercenaries hired by the British during the Revolutionary War, described the area in his diary. In 1778, he said the river was "constantly full of ships, of which those of medium size can sail up to the city. In this city, especially in times of peace, there is always a surplus of items necessary to provide a comfortable life."

Today, Philadelphia's nautical heritage comes alive at the Independence Seaport Museum, the popular centerpiece of Penn's Landing, where you can see maritime artifacts, interactive exhibits and ship models. Then tour the real thing: the *USS Olympia*, flagship at the Battle of Manila Bay in the Spanish-American War; the *USS Becuna*, a World War II submarine; the *Gazela*, the oldest and largest wooden square-rigger still sailing; and the *USS New Jersey*, a highly decorated battleship, open to the public on the Camden waterfront.

The waters along Penn's Landing are busy once again with traffic of all kinds. Dozens of pleasure-boaters glide in and out of the marina. Tugs and cargo vessels chug by, and a paddlewheel riverboat and cruise vessels ply the waters, as their passengers dance, enjoy meals and tour the waterfront. Those more interested in what

Penn's Landing

lies beneath the waters can take a ferry boat across the river to the Adventure Aquarium in Camden. Nearby is the simple clapboard rowhouse of poet Walt Whitman and the BB&T Pavilion, an outdoor amphitheater/indoor theater complex.

Back at Penn's Landing, concerts, festivals and fireworks take place all year long. In the past, they were held at a large outdoor amphitheater called the Great Plaza. But plans call for the capping of I-95 from Walnut Street to Chestnut to help bridge Center City and the waterfront, more public green space, hundreds of new housing units and hotel rooms, and tens of thousands of square feet of retail, restaurants and entertainment. The area hosts about 70 events from May through September, including concerts and multicultural festivals.

The Tour

❶ Begin Walk 4 along the eastern edge of Society Hill (Walk 3) at the **Philadelphia Vietnam Veterans Memorial (1)** (*Columbus Boulevard and Spruce Street*). The memorial honors 648 Philadelphians who died in the Vietnam War. It was dedicated in 1987 and has been recognized for its architectural style. Scenes of the war are captured on the polished granite walls, calling to mind the sacrifices of American service men and women in Southeast Asia. In this peaceful amphitheater-like setting, amid trees and landscaped brick walkways, visitors pause and remember.

❷ Leaving the memorial, walk east on cobblestoned Spruce Street, cross Columbus Boulevard and enter the former **International Sculpture Garden (2)** (*Columbus Boulevard and Spruce Streets*), an attractive, tree-shaded park where you'll find benches, water spouts from Indonesia and a monument commemorating the achievements of Christopher Columbus. Several sculptures were moved into storage to clear the way for nearby development. The tall, narrow Columbus monument rises overhead like a church tower. The park is adjacent to the busy marina, where pleasure boats come and go.

❸ The eye is quickly drawn to a large ship, the **USS Olympia (3)** (*Penn's Landing at Spruce Street*), the flagship at the Battle of Manila Bay during the Spanish-American War and the last surviving vessel of the war. (Open seven days a week from March 19 to September 30. Check website for hours. Also open 10 a.m. to 3 p.m. Wednesday through Friday and 10 a.m. to 5 p.m. on Saturday and Sunday from October through December and from March 1 to 19; and 10 a.m. to 5 p.m. on Saturday and Sunday from January through February.) Tickets $18 for adults and $14 for seniors, 65 and older, and children, 3 to 17. The price includes admission to the World War II submarine *USS Becuna* (Stop 4) and to Independence Seaport Museum (Stop 5).

A century ago, the *Olympia* was the state-of-the-art flagship of the U.S. Navy, a key player in the Spanish-American War and a source of great national pride for a country flexing its muscles. On its bridge, Commodore George Dewey uttered those famous words—"You may fire when you are ready, Gridley"—during the Battle of Manila Bay.

USS Olympia

The *Olympia*'s mighty guns announced the United States as an international power. In the battle on May 1, 1898, the *Olympia* led five other American warships, which destroyed 10 Spanish cruisers and gunboats in a few hours without losing an American life. The action helped wrest the Philippines from the Spanish.

Today, the vessel is operated by the Independence Seaport Museum. The museum took over the *Olympia* on January 1, 1996, from the Olympia Cruiser Association, which had tried to maintain the vessel with limited resources for 40 years. The ship has been undergoing restoration and refurbishing in recent years. Visitors can tour the whole ship, from the engine room and galley to the gun batteries, pilothouse and officers' staterooms. The vessel has a rich collection of paintings, photographs and artifacts that will thrill maritime history buffs.

❹ Alongside the *Olympia* is a smaller but no less interesting vessel from another conflict: the **USS Becuna (4)** (*Penn's Landing at Spruce Street*), a 318-foot-long, guppy-class submarine used during World War II. (Open 10 a.m. to 3 p.m. Wednesday through Friday and 10 a.m. to 5 p.m. Saturday and Sunday.) Tickets $18 for adults and $14 for seniors, 65 and older, and children, 3 to 17. The price includes admission to the *Olympia* (Stop 3) and Independence Seaport Museum (Stop 5).

The *Becuna* conducted search-and-destroy missions in the South Pacific in the 1940s and was once filled with crewmen scurrying up and down ladders and narrow walkways. Today, adults and children follow the same paths as they examine claustrophobic quarters, scan the instruments and listen to guides describe life onboard the vessel.

❺ Leaving the *Becuna*, stroll north along the edge of the marina to the **Independence Seaport Museum (5)** (*211 South Columbus Boulevard at Walnut Street*). This is the riverfront's premier attraction, offering a glimpse of Philadelphia's maritime past as well as interactive exhibits that will delight children and adults alike. (Open 10 a.m. to 5 p.m. daily. Closed Thanksgiving, Christmas and New Year's Day.) Tickets $18 for adults and $14 for seniors, 65 and older, and children, 3 to 17. The price includes admission to the *Olympia* (Stop 3) and the World War II submarine, *USS Becuna* (Stop 4).

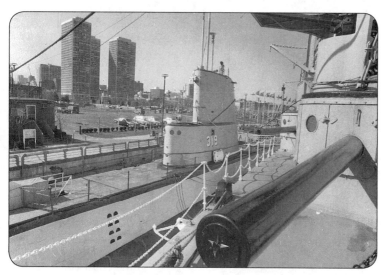

USS Becuna

Inside are educational and entertaining exhibits that tell the story of the Delaware River's impact on the city's history. In the "Patriots and Pirates" exhibit, tour the Diligence, a full-size replica of a schooner similar to those that played a crucial role in protecting American merchant ships from attacks by Britain, France and the Barbary pirates at the end of the 18th century. Also see intricate ship models and maritime artifacts.

6 Outside the museum is the passenger terminal for the **RiverLink Ferry (6)** (*Penn's Landing near Walnut Street*). Roundtrip tickets cost $9 for ages 13 to 65, $7 for age 65 and older and children 3 to 12. The fare is free to those under age 2. The operation season runs May through October. (Not a car ferry.)

7 The ferry provides a brief, pleasant ride—in the protected interior or on the breezy deck—across the Delaware River to the **Adventure Aquarium (7)** (*1 South Riverside Drive in Camden*). The

Penguins at
Adventure
Aquarium

aquarium is home to 15,000 species of marine life throughout two million gallons of water and has the largest collection of sharks on the East Coast. (Open 9:30 a.m. to 4 p.m. Monday through Friday, and 9:30 a.m. to 5 p.m. on Saturday and Sunday. Admission is $34.11 per adult. Each child, 2–12, accompanied by an adult, is free. Otherwise, admission for children is $25.58.)

Here you'll see African blackfooted penguins, ferocious-looking sharks, bizarre fish from Madagascar, playful seals, sea turtles and stingrays. Ask a diver questions—over a scubaphone—as he floats in the ocean tank. Watch the daily penguin feedings. And pet a small shark gliding through a shallow tank. The aquarium is as much fun for adults as it is for children.

The aquarium has the largest collection of sharks on the East Coast, including the only great hammerhead shark on exhibit in the United States. It's also the only aquarium to exhibit hippos and one of six to have Little Blue penguins as permanent residents.

8 Nearby is the **Camden Children's Garden (8)** (*Riverside Drive adjacent to the Adventure Aquarium*), which provides themed garden exhibits and hands-on activities that help children learn about the environment and horticulture. (Open 10 a.m. to 3 p.m. Wednesday through Friday, and 10 a.m. to 4 p.m. Saturday and Sunday. Closed to the public during January, February and March. Admission to the garden is $9; Camden city residents with valid ID, $6; and infants age 1 and under, free.)

Visit two indoor attractions: the popular Philadelphia Eagles Four Seasons Butterfly House, and the tropical exhibit, Plaza de Aibonito. Other exhibits include a Dinosaur Garden with prehistoric animals fashioned from recycled auto parts, a Maze, Tree House, Picnic Garden, CityScapes Garden, Storybook Gardens and the Fitness Garden. Visitors can also ride the carousel and train.

Camden Children's Garden

Walt Whitman's House

9 A few blocks away is **Walt Whitman's house (9)** (*330 Mickle Boulevard, also known as Dr. Martin Luther King Jr. Boulevard and as Mickle Street in Whitman's time*), the only house ever owned by the famed poet. Walk south on Riverside Drive toward Mickle/King Boulevard, turn left there and follow it to the house. (Open for house tours 10 a.m. to noon and 1 to 4 p.m. Wednesday through Saturday, and 1 to 4 p.m. on Sunday. To tour, just knock on the door. Admission is free.)

Whitman bought this Greek Revival rowhouse—"a little shanty of my own"—in 1884, paying $1,750 for it. Today, it's a shrine, filled with the poet's belongings: his knapsack, leather slippers and bone-tipped oak cane. Some of the items are on display in rooms that have been restored to the way they looked when Whitman lived here. The light fixtures, the wallpaper, rugs and other treatments have been duplicated, using photos of the rooms from the poet's time. Dishes once used by Whitman sit on a table in the kitchen. Many artifacts have survived, including Whitman's large, round, gray-brown felt hat, his personal letters, a cast of his left hand, even the handwritten death notice that was tacked to his front door when he died.

Whitman's big, wooden rocker sits next to a window in the front parlor. The sill of the window was extended, apparently so Whitman could use it to write on. A photo of his father is on the wall, and a statue of Grover Cleveland stands on the floor next to the fireplace. Here the poet received visitors, sometimes taking them on a carriage ride to view his massive tomb under construction a few miles away at Harleigh Cemetery, in the 1600 block of Haddon Avenue. Upstairs is the oak bed in which Whitman died on March 26, 1892.

⓾ Head west on Mickle/King Boulevard to the Delaware River, then south along the waterfront to the **battleship New Jersey (10)** (*62 Battleship Place, berthed south of Wiggins Park Marina*), one of the most decorated warships in United States history. (Admission charged.)

Guided tours of the battleship include a visit to the ship's combat engagement center, with all of its electronic gear, as well as the famous 16-inch guns and cruise missiles. Visitors also will view quarters and eating areas of the officers and sailors who served on the ship through four wars. As you leave the ship, stop by a gift shop of naval mementos at the end of the pier.

⓫ Head back to the RiverLink ferry, cross over to Penn's Landing, then head north along the river to the **Gazela (11)** (*100 block of S. Columbus Boulevard at Penn's Landing*), a 177-foot square-rigger that has served as the Port of Philadelphia's goodwill ambassador.

Gazela

(Open daily when the ship is in port. Tours upon request. Call ahead: 215-238-0280. Donations accepted.)

The graceful ship was built in 1901, the last of a Portuguese fleet of fishing vessels. It has sailed up and down the Atlantic Coast, representing Philadelphia at festivals and celebrations, but has remained closer to home more recently, visiting places such as Lewes and Wilmington, Delaware. Upgrades must be made before it can be cleared by the Coast Guard for ocean voyages. While in port, the *Gazela* is rented for events including weddings and business meetings.

12 If *you* would like to experience some sailing—along with historical narration, dining and musical entertainment—cruise ships are available along Penn's Landing, including the **Spirit of Philadelphia, Ben Franklin Yacht** and **Freedom Elite Yacht (12)**. (Details mentioned earlier in this walk.)

13 One of the historical sites pointed out during cruises is **Fort Mifflin (13)** (*1 Fort Mifflin Road near Island Road and Hog Island Road on the Delaware River, next to Philadelphia International Airport*). It was here that a few hundred patriots endured the greatest naval bombardment of the Revolutionary War and held off British forces for nearly two months while Washington's army moved to Valley Forge. If you want to visit by car, get on Interstate 95 at Penn's Landing and follow it south to Island Avenue. (Open 10 a.m. to 4 p.m. Wednesday to Sunday, from March 1 through December 15. Tours 11 a.m., 1 p.m. and 3 p.m. Admission is $8, $6 for seniors, $4 for children 6 to 12 and free for children 5 and under. For more information, call 215-685-4167.)

Fort Mifflin was named for its builder, Gen. Thomas Mifflin, who would later sign the Constitution. It was erected in the 1770s on tiny Mud Island to isolate the troops from the peaceful Quaker city of Philadelphia. Here, in the fall of 1777, American troops withstood a withering artillery barrage, sometimes up to 1,000 cannon shots an hour. In the damp cold, without adequate clothing or blankets, the men took cover wherever they could from the shots that came from every direction. Private Johann Conrad Dohla, one of 30,000 Hessian mercenaries hired by the British, described the fighting in his diary: "The warships *Somerset, Experiment* and *Vigilant* sailed farther up the river very early this morning, and they fired at Mud Island and Fort Mifflin, which are strongly occupied by the enemy," he wrote on November 13, 1777. "The cannonade from these three ships lasted

Parade at Fort Mifflin

continuously for three days and nights, and in this time there must have been more than twelve thousand shots fired on both sides."

The stakes were high. The British could not hold the city, much less pursue the Continental Army under George Washington, if they could not ship supplies up the Delaware to their 18,000 troops in Philadelphia. Washington told the commander of the fort, Gen. James Mitchell Varnum, to hold on "to the last extremity." Yet Washington was not willing to sacrifice the troops for an attempt at forcing the British to evacuate Philadelphia. He expected Varnum's troops to leave Mud Island before the fort was destroyed. The battle was part of a campaign that included Delaware River clashes at Red Bank and Paulsboro, New Jersey. At Mifflin, the British ships were forced by chevaux-de-frise, iron-tipped logs set in the river to sink or disable enemy vessels, to sail into the fort's line of fire.

The thundering guns of the Royal Navy and land batteries shook the buildings in Philadelphia and were heard across South Jersey. Shells breached the wood palisades and stone wall and severely damaged three blockhouses. While their flag was still flying over the fort, about 300 soldiers were evacuated on three boats that took them to safety in New Jersey. They took 20 bodies but had to leave 50 behind. But the British, by their own estimation, had lost two of the most precious months of the war, along with several large warships.

After the Revolution, Fort Mifflin became part of a system of coastal and harbor defenses in the new republic, and it was later used as a military prison and storage facility during the Civil War. One of the prisoners at the fort, a deserter who killed an officer during the Civil War, was hanged here. Mifflin was repeatedly repaired and modified, though its architectural shape remained unchanged. The Army abandoned it in the 1950s, and preservationists turned it into a historic attraction.

Today, the fort remains isolated, though it is no longer on an island. The narrow channel that separated it from the Pennsylvania mainland has filled in over the years. The site is now obscured by the high grasses of a wildlife sanctuary. Tugboats and ships glide by and jetliners pass directly overheard. But with help from authentically dressed guides, visitors have no trouble leaving the present for a trip back in time.

Walk the parade ground. Tour the museum, the restored officers' quarters, soldiers' barracks and bomb shelter. Then look past the cannon and walls to the river, where the mighty British fleet once laid siege, and imagine what took place here more than two centuries ago.

14 If you want an escape of another kind, take a side trip to the **John Heinz National Wildlife Refuge at Tinicum (14)** (*8601 Lindbergh Boulevard and 86th Street*). The refuge covers a 1,200-acre freshwater tidal marsh that is a migratory stopover or home to at least 300 species of birds—ducks, geese, egrets, herons—as well as a host of land animals, such as deer, raccoons, foxes, turtles and weasels. The largest refuge of its kind in the state, it is near Philadelphia International Airport and convenient to Interstate 95, which can be accessed at Penn's Landing. (Open daily from sunrise to sunset. The visitor center is open from 9 a.m. to 4 p.m. daily. No admission charge.)

Three hundred years ago, the area was teeming with life. Native Americans called it the "Islands of the Marsh," a series of scattered islands and streams across 6,000 acres. By the 1630s, the new settlers had diked the marshes to make pastureland. In the 1900s, real estate developers transformed the area into an industrial park. And in the 1950s, the Army Corps of Engineers started dumping mud dredged from the shipping channel of the Delaware River, shrinking the marsh. But Congress voted to save the marsh in 1972, declaring

John Heinz National Wildlife Refuge at Tinicum

it a wildlife refuge. Since then, efforts have been underway to restore the wetlands.

The effort has paid off. This preserve is perfect for hikers, bird-watchers and nature lovers. The area includes eight miles of foot trails, a canoe launch into Darby Creek and an observation deck. If you're game for more walking, the peaceful scenes here will rejuvenate the spirit.

Southwark: A Stroll Through Time

Southwark: A Stroll Through Time

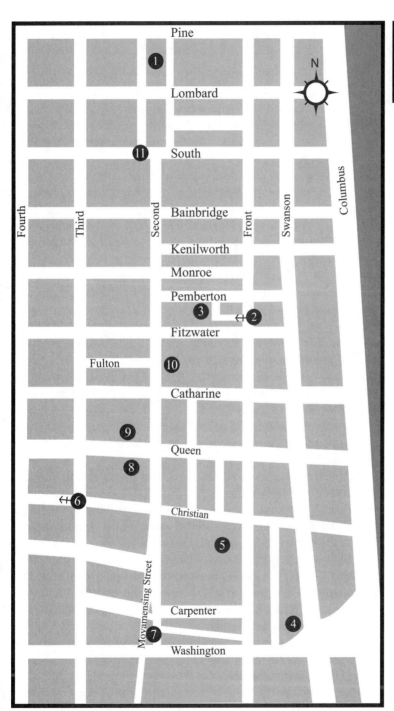

> ### USEFUL INFORMATION
>
> Southwark is bounded on the north by Lombard Street, on the south by Carpenter Street, on the west by Sixth Street and on the east by Swanson Street. In that general area are several good restaurants including South Street Diner, 140 South Street, and the Southwark Restaurant, 701 South Fourth Street.
>
> Parking is available at Second and Lombard Streets and at Third and Lombard Streets. Numerous metered parking spaces also are available.
>
> The city's transit system (SEPTA) runs buses through the area. (See transportation information in Walk 1 for details.)

Introduction

One of the oldest sections of Philadelphia, Southwark was known by another name before it was settled by the English. Native Americans who lived here in a village along the Delaware River called it *Wicaco*—a name adopted by the Swedes when they arrived in the mid-1600s.

The new arrivals began a settlement on land patented by Sweden's Queen Christina and were firmly established in the area by the 1660s. They built a log blockhouse for the protection of their fellow countrymen in 1669 and modified it for use as a church in 1675. The influence of these early settlers can still be seen in the names of the streets—Swanson, Queen and Christian—and in the building of Gloria Dei, the present Old Swedes' Church, which was dedicated in 1700 as the settlement grew north and west.

At the time William Penn's advance party arrived, only a few hundred European colonists lived within the boundaries of today's Philadelphia. That changed after Penn landed in 1682. Within two years, the town had hundreds of new residents, along with shops, a school, municipal government, a jail and a court system. The English bought land along the riverfront south of South Street for stores and warehouses. By the middle of the 18th century, the area had become known as Southwark, after the London borough south of the Thames. It became the center of a bustling and thriving shipbuilding industry that made Philadelphia the largest port of the colonies and of the new United States.

The abundant supply of wood and skilled labor enabled the development of shipyards in Southwark, where merchant ships and men-of-war were turned out. The first United States Navy Yard was located a few blocks south of Old Swedes' Church. Like its namesake in London, the area was home to merchants, shipwrights, pilots, riggers and sailors, who lived in small, simple, wood-frame houses. Even today, Southwark has the flavor of that old seafaring community. Hundreds of houses, built by working men in the 18th century, still stand—some grown larger with additions.

Philadelphians, then as now, had a taste for entertainment. Southwark was the site of the city's first playhouses. The Quakers stopped such amusements in the city proper, but Lewis Hallam's company of players gave a performance in a warehouse in 1754. And the Southwark Theatre opened in 1759 as a permanent place of theatrical productions. The Hallam company put on shows there until 1790.

The concentration of people in Southwark made it one of the hardest-hit areas during the cholera epidemic of 1832. More than 2,300 cases were reported in the city and nearly 1,000 people died. One in 70 Philadelphians was stricken, and one in 173 perished.

Newcomers continued to settle in Southwark in the mid-19th century as the housing there began showing signs of decay. An 1840 map by engineer Charles Ellet Jr. shows Philadelphia's built-up area extending from the Delaware River west to Sixth Street and from the Navy Yard in Southwark north to the private yards in Kensington. The city had a population at the time of more than 258,000.

The population swelled during the Civil War as tens of thousands of troops flowed through the city on trains, ships and barges. In 1861, a grocer and fruit dealer, Barzilai S. Brown, helped distribute free refreshments to the troops passing through the Navy Yard. He leased a small boat shop at Swanson Street and Washington Avenue as a "free refreshment saloon for soldiers." The troops initially called it "Brown's," but it was officially organized as the "Union Volunteer Refreshment Saloon" on May 27, 1861. Buildings were added over time until full regiments were provided with washing facilities and meals.

One soldier wrote to his parents on June 1, 1863, describing the fine treatment he had received in Philadelphia. "I know that my pen cannot half do justice to the subject but I know that the remembrance of it will live in the hearts of our brave artillery boys as long as they are able to train a gun or draw a sword in the defence [sic] of their country," he wrote. "Anyone who thinks there is any lack of support for the war has only to march through Philadelphia."

The Tour

❶ Begin at **Head House Square (1)** (*Second and Pine Streets*), visited on Walk 3. Using it as a starting point, head south on Second Street, cross South Street, turn left at Bainbridge Street and right on Front Street. Walk south on Front, passing Kenilworth, Monroe and Pemberton Streets.

❷ Between Pemberton and Fitzwater, look at the unique collection of brick houses called **Workman Place (2)** (*742–744 Front Street at Pemberton Street*), built by John Workman in 1812 and now maintained by the Octavia Hill Association as low-cost housing. (Not open to the public.)

❸ Follow Pemberton Street to the **Mifflin Houses (3)** (*Pemberton Street between Front and Second Streets*), two historic brick buildings that still proudly proclaim their owner's name and the date of their construction. (Not open to the public.)

On the upper wall you'll see the initials "G.M." on one and "1748" on the other. The initials stand for George Mifflin, grandfather of Thomas Mifflin, the Revolutionary War general who built Fort Mifflin and who was a governor of Pennsylvania. The houses face each other beyond brick walls and a small iron gateway. They again remind visitors of the area's British roots. Inside the gate is a picturesque, tree-shaded courtyard.

❹ Walk south on Front Street, turn left (east) on Christian Street, then right (south) on Swanson Street to **Gloria Dei**, or **Old Swedes' Church (4)** (*916 Swanson Street*), the oldest church in Pennsylvania. (Open 9 a.m. to 4 p.m. Tuesday through Sunday. Call first: 215-389-1513. No admission fee. Services at 10 a.m. on Sunday.)

The church was organized in 1646. Its members initially met in a wood frame building in Tinicum but moved to a crude log blockhouse at the current location. Work on the present church began in 1698. The charming brick structure was built by John Smart, John

Old Swedes' Church

Harrison and John Brett, and completed in 1700. Here, Betsy Ross, the widow of John Ross, married Capt. Joseph Ashbourn on June 15, 1777. At the time, Gloria Dei was much closer to the busy Delaware River. Photographs from 1854 show the steeple rising into the sky and the tall masts of ships almost directly to its rear. Over the centuries, the land has been filled in—and now traffic flows by on Delaware Avenue where sailing vessels once docked.

Gloria Dei, popularly known as Old Swedes' Church, is flanked by trees and a graveyard, giving it a tranquil, picturesque setting that has stood the test of time. The church that once served a Swedish Lutheran congregation is now an Episcopal church and historic site, with several noteworthy relics. Make sure to see the venerable carvings of cherubim with an open Bible on the balcony. They date back to the church's earliest beginnings. Hanging from the ceiling are models of two ships that carried Swedish settlers here in 1638.

Outside in the churchyard is the grave of Alexander Wilson, the father of American ornithology, who asked to be buried here. Wilson, a native of Paisley, Scotland, liked the spot because it was a quiet place, he said, where the birds would always sing. Adjacent to the church and graveyard is the parish hall, the caretaker's house, the rectory and the Roak house, which displays lightning rods designed and produced by Benjamin Franklin for the church.

To learn more about the contributions of the Swedish people, visit the **American Swedish Historical Museum**, 1900 Pattison Avenue in South Philadelphia. The museum is built on land granted to Swedish settlers in 1653 and housed in a 17th-century-style manor house. (The museum is open 10 a.m. to 4 p.m. from Tuesday to Friday and noon to 4 p.m. on Saturday and Sunday. Admission is $10 for adults, $7 for seniors and students, and $5 for children ages 5 to 11.)

5 Follow Christian Street west to Front Street, turn left and walk one block to Carpenter Street, where you'll see a rare sight looming overhead: a 142-foot brick **Shot Tower (5)** (*Front Street*

Shot Tower

between Christian and Carpenter Streets). The first of its kind constructed in the United States, it was erected by John Bishop and Thomas Sparks in 1807 and used for 100 years. Shot was poured into molds, and while cooling was dropped from the height of the tower into water. The area around the tower is now a recreation center and playground.

6 For a side trip, walk west on Christian Street to the **Italian Market (6)** (*Ninth Street between Christian and Wharton Streets*), a bustling, open-air marketplace where vendors crowd the sidewalks with their food and goods. (Outdoor vendors open 7 a.m. to 7 p.m. Monday through Saturday, and 8 a.m. to 1 p.m. on Sunday. Many food stalls are closed on Mondays, but the majority of stores and restaurants are open.)

The market was established by Italian immigrants in the late 19th century and offers visitors fresh pasta, fruits, vegetables and imported items found nowhere else. You'll also find wonderful pastry, cheese and bread shops and several Italian restaurants nearby. Many people remember the market from the scene in the movie *Rocky*, where the fighter jogs down the street.

7 Walk south on Ninth Street, then east on Washington Street to Second Street for another worthwhile side trip—to the

A deli in the Italian Market

Mummers Museum

Mummers Museum (7) (*1100 South Second Street at Washington*). This unusual local institution presents the history of the Mummers, the guys who dress up in feathered finery and march in Philadelphia's New Year's Day parade. (Open 9:30 a.m. to 4 p.m. Wednesday through Saturday. Admission is free. Free concerts are held, weather permitting, at 8 p.m. on Thursdays from May through September.)

The English colonists dressed in costumes and performed pantomimes at Christmas. That custom caught on in Philadelphia, where families held costume parties on New Year's Day. Some groups of costumed revelers paraded on the streets on the first day of the centennial year, 1876, and Mummery was born. Today, there are dozens of clubs competing for cash prizes.

8 Leaving the Mummers Museum, head north on Second Street to Queen Street, where you'll come to **St. Philip Neri Church (8)** (*218 Queen Street between Second and Third Streets*), a handsome Greek Revival church built in 1840. (Masses are celebrated at 7:30 a.m. Thursday and Friday, 8 a.m. on Saturday and 11 a.m. on Sunday. A vigil is held at 4:30 p.m. on Saturday. Visitors welcome. During the afternoon, check at the rectory next door.)

St. Philip Neri Church

The church was designed by Napoleon Le Brun, who worked in the office of Thomas Ustick Walter, a famous architect. Le Brun designed St. Philip Neri Church at the age of 19, before leaving Walter's employ to open his own office. "IHS" (the first three letters of the Greek name for Jesus, used as a Christian symbol or monogram, and also viewed as the initial letters of a Latin phrase meaning "in this sign you will conquer") and "A.D. 1840" are emblazoned in gold over the main entrance, and a cross rises above the pediment.

Inside is a beautiful fresco of the Resurrection and an altarpiece depicting the Creation by the Italian painter Nicola Monachesi. The church was targeted by anti-Irish mobs in 1844. Irish immigration had increased dramatically in the first half of the 19th century, and the traditional religious tolerance broke down as native-born Americans lost their jobs to the newcomers.

9 Across the street from the church is the small, tree-shaded **Mario Lanza Park (9)** (*200 block of Queen Street*). It was dedicated in 1967 to the memory of the famous tenor and actor who lived nearby in the 600 block of Christian Street and will always be re-

Bust of Mario Lanza at Mario Lanza Institute and Museum

membered in South Philadelphia. Take a break here on a bench, amid flower planters and towering sycamores. Green and gray banners are emblazoned with the image of the singer and the name of the park.

Several blocks away is the **Mario Lanza Institute and Museum**, which relocated in 2019 to 12th and Reed Streets. The museum pays tribute to Lanza with displays of posters, paintings, clippings, costumes, photos and a life-sized terra-cotta bust of Lanza along with other memorabilia, including films that play on a large-screen television. The great tenor lives on here. Nearby at Broad and Reed Streets is a giant outside wall mural of Lanza. (Museum admission is $10. Call 215-238-9691 or go to www.mariolanzainstitute.org for more information on hours.)

10 Head east on Queen Street to Second Street, turn left and walk to the former **Southwark Baptist Church (10)** (*771 South Second Street between Catherine and Fitzwater Streets*), the first all-stone structure in the Southwark area. (Not open to the public.)

South Street

The small, gray building, fronted by a decorative, wrought-iron fence and set back from the street, was constructed about 1810 by the Third Baptist Church. It was the Southwark Baptist Church from 1810 to 1898, subsequently was occupied by the Polish National Society, then was purchased and refurbished in 1905 by the Congregation Ahavas Achim Nazin Misach Hoarce, a group of Jews from Nezine, Poland. The building became the Neziner Synagogue and later, in the 1980s, was purchased and converted to condominiums.

11 Walk north on Second Street toward Head House Square, then turn left onto **South Street (11)**. You're now in the Greenwich Village of Philadelphia—South Street. On this strip, from Front to 10th Street, you'll find scores of restaurants, theaters, nightclubs, art galleries and shops, both funky and elegant. We'll leave you here to relax with a drink at an outdoor café and watch the passing parade.

Washington Square West

Washington Square West

1. Independence Square
2. Washington Square
3. Athenaeum of Philadelphia
4. Penn Mutual Life Insurance Building
5. Curtis Center and The Dream Garden
6. Asaph Stone House
7. Christopher Morley House
8. Lea & Febiger Building
9. Holy Trinity Catholic Church
10. Birthplace of Joseph Jefferson
11. Home of Nicholas Biddle
12. Church of St. George
13. Musical Fund Hall
14. Reynolds-Morris House
15. Walnut Street Theatre
16. Bonaparte House
17. Mikveh Israel Cemetery
18. Sarah Josepha Hale House
19. Pennsylvania Hospital
20. Treaty Elm
21. Mother Bethel African Methodist Episcopal Church

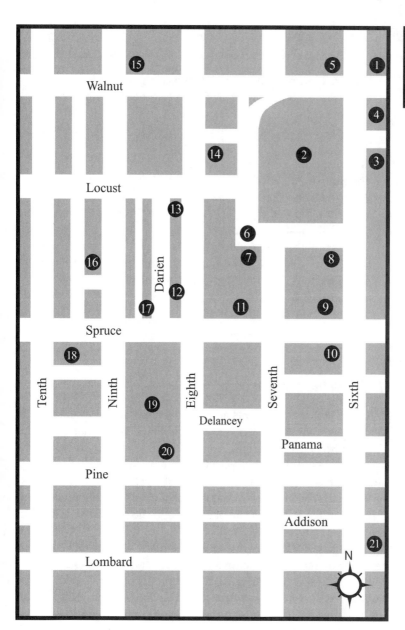

Walnut

Locust

Darien

Spruce

Tenth

Ninth

Eighth

Delancey

Seventh

Sixth

Panama

Pine

Addison

Lombard

N

USEFUL INFORMATION

Washington Square is bounded on the east by Sixth Street, on the west by Seventh Street, on the north by Walnut Street and on the south by Locust Street. Our walk also will take us west of the square into the neighborhood known as Washington Square West. Among the nearby restaurants, pubs and eateries worth noting are the Food Hall at The Bourse, 111 South Independence Mall East (mentioned in Walk 1); Ocean City Restaurant, 234 North Ninth Street; Penang (Malaysian cuisine), 117 North 10th Street; and Fergie's Pub, 1214 Sansom Street.

Parking is available at Seventh and Clinton Streets, Eighth and Clinton Streets, Eighth and Walnut Streets, and Eighth and Chestnut Streets. Numerous metered parking spaces also are available. The city's transit system, SEPTA, services the area. (See Walk 1 for details.)

Introduction

Washington Square was an open pasture before it was set aside more than 300 years ago as one of the five squares in William Penn's original plan for Philadelphia. Over the centuries, it has served widely different roles. It has been a mass burial ground for soldiers of the Revolution and victims of a yellow fever epidemic. It has been the center of the city's most fashionable neighborhood. And it has been the hallowed site of a shrine to the soldiers who died in the war for independence.

Some historic buildings along the square have been razed and replaced by modern structures. The south side once was graced by the First Presbyterian Church, a well-proportioned Greek Revival building designed by architect John Haviland in the 1820s. Today the Hopkinson House, a high-rise condominium building, is on the site. On the east side of the square, two 19th-century houses were replaced by a colonial-style house (225 South Sixth Street) once occupied by Richardson Dilworth, mayor of Philadelphia in the late 1950s. A plaque with the mayor's likeness is affixed to a slab of black marble next to the house.

But the community retains many treasures. Generations of Philadelphians have closely guarded them, generally choosing to restore or incorporate the past into the present. Washington Square's tall, spreading trees and Federal-era houses at the southwest end lend a certain elegance to this area of the city, which has the feel of many eras imprinted on it.

In our walk, we will tread through the remnants of these other times. We will visit the homes of the rich and famous, august publishing houses and historic churches. So slip into some comfortable walking shoes—and let's go.

The Tour

①-② Starting at the southwest corner of **Independence Square (1)** (*Sixth and Walnut Streets*), cross Sixth, then Walnut. You're now in the northeast corner of **Washington Square (2)** (*Sixth and Walnut Streets*). It was known originally as "the southeast square" by Quakers, who eschewed conferring honors on people by naming places after them. It was renamed Washington Square in 1833.

Laid out as a city square typical of those found in London, this historic ground became the burial place for 2,000 American and British soldiers of the Revolution, as well as for many victims of the yellow fever epidemic of 1793. As you stroll down the walkway at the northeast corner of the park, notice a plaque honoring American soldiers who died in jails in Philadelphia after being imprisoned here during the British occupation in 1777 and 1778. Nearby is a marker honoring a sycamore tree that grew from a seed carried to the moon in 1971 on *Apollo 14*; the seed was planted on May 6, 1975. The original tree died, but it was replaced with a clone in 2011.

Further on is the **memorial tomb to the "Unknown Soldiers of the Revolution,"** recalling the sacrifice of the early patriots. "Freedom is a light for which many men have died in darkness," an inscription says. "In unmarked graves within this square lie thousands of unknown soldiers of Washington's Army who died of wounds and sickness during the Revolutionary War." In Washington's farewell address on September 17, 1796, part of which is engraved here, the commander-in-chief reminded his countrymen of freedom's cost: "The independence and liberty you possess are the work of joint councils and joint efforts—of common dangers, sufferings and success."

Memorial Tomb to the "Unknown Soldiers of the Revolution" in Washington Square

Standing at the fountain in the center of the square, imagine the changes that have taken place here over the years. On the east side of the square stood the notorious Walnut Street Prison. It ran along Sixth Street, from Walnut to Locust. At the end of the 18th century, its most famous inmate was Robert Morris, financier of the Revolution, who wound up imprisoned for being unable to pay his own debts. If you had been in the square in 1793, you would have seen Jean-Pierre Blanchard ascend in a balloon from the prison yard. George Washington and hundreds of others watched America's first aeronaut.

By the middle of the 19th century, the square had taken on a more residential character. It was flanked by elegant houses, frequented by Philadelphia's most influential citizens, and soon became the center of the city's most affluent neighborhood. This attractive park underwent $2.6 million in paving restorations at the end of the 20th century.

❸ On the east side of the square is the **Athenaeum of Philadelphia (3)** (*219 South Sixth Street*), an imposing brownstone that houses a research library with splendid collections of materials on architecture, decoration and design. (Open 9 a.m. to 5 p.m. Monday through Friday. All tours and research are by appointment only. Phone 215-925-2688.)

Athenaeum of Philadelphia

The Athenaeum was founded as a proprietary library, and its present building was designed in 1845 by architect John Notman. His dignified-looking structure introduced the Italian Renaissance Revival style to the United States. It was to have been built of marble, but was switched to brownstone to save on costs. The gas lamps out front add to its air of the past. In the rear of the building, notice the small, attractive garden and the ironwork on the second-floor porch.

The Athenaeum was a peculiarly Victorian institution: a private library supported by people who wanted access to the latest books and periodicals in a comfortable and elegant clubhouse atmosphere. It has a large collection of materials on the French in America and on early travel in this country.

But the library's most significant role today is as the single most important repository for drawings and other documents on Philadelphia architecture. A National Historic Landmark, the Athenaeum has used some of its resources for commercial ventures to help support the institution. It licenses a line of 19th-century wallpaper designs from its collections.

Inside, the Athenaeum is filled with notable paintings, statuary and fine period furniture. There's a magnificent wood stairway with banisters of cast iron, an elegant Empire pier table and magnificent portraits by artist John Neagle.

4 Leave the quiet of the library now and walk next door to the **Penn Mutual Life Insurance Building (4)** (*Sixth and Walnut Streets*), a modern office building with an Egyptian Revival facade by John Haviland. The architect's original building at this site was razed, but the facade on Walnut Street was preserved and made part of the new tower.

5 Now cross Walnut Street for an unforgettable treat. Step inside the lobby of the **Curtis Center (5)** (*Sixth and Walnut Streets*), former home of Curtis Publishing Company and site of an artistic masterpiece.

Here is a reminder of the days when Philadelphia was an important center of magazine publishing. The Curtis Publishing Company put out *The Saturday Evening Post, Ladies' Home Journal, Country Gentleman* and *Holiday*—general-interest magazines that provided mass entertainment in the days before television.

Here, too, is a stunning work of art: **The Dream Garden (5)**, a Maxfield Parrish glass mosaic mural that is 15 feet high by 50 feet long. (Open for viewing 8 a.m. to 6 p.m. Monday through Friday and 10 a.m. to 1 p.m. Saturday. Closed Sunday.) This unusual work was created by the Louis C. Tiffany Studios, based on an original painting by Parrish. It has 260 color tones and is made up of thousands of pieces of luminous glass.

The Dream Garden

6 Leaving the Curtis Center, walk toward the southwest corner of Washington Square. A group of historic houses provides an idea of how this area used to look. Note the former **Asaph Stone House (6)** (*702 South Washington Square, near Seventh Street*), a magnificent 19th-century house once owned by wealthy Philadelphia merchant Asaph Stone. (Not open to the public.) The house was constructed between 1818 and 1821 in the Greek Revival style. Notice the fanlight over the doorway.

7 Three houses from the corner is the one-time home of novelist, journalist and social commentator **Christopher Morley (7)** (*704 South Washington Square, near Seventh Street*), who lived here before he became famous for such works as *Kitty Foyle* (1939) and *Parnassus on Wheels* (1917). As a young man living on Washington Square, Morley watched the swells of Philadelphia society and wrote scathing commentary about them. Like the Asaph Stone House, this one has a fanlight adorning the doorway. (Not open to the public.)

8 On South Washington Square, walk past the Hopkinson House to the former **Lea & Febiger Building (8)** (*600 South Washington Square*), an elegant Italianate Palazzo-style structure. America's oldest publishing house, Lea & Febiger was founded in 1785 by Matthew Carey. As Carey, Lea & Blanchard, the firm became the publishers of many famous authors, including Charles Dickens, Edgar Allan Poe and Washington Irving. An art gallery is open here from 10 a.m. to 6 p.m. Tuesday through Saturday.

9 Make a right turn on Sixth Street and head south to **Holy Trinity Catholic Church (9)** (*Sixth and Spruce Streets*), which opened in 1789 with a German congregation. The church later created the first Catholic orphan asylum in America. (Masses on Sunday. Call ahead for tours: 215-923-7930.)

The churchyard held the remains of 19th-century banker and philanthropist Stephen Girard until they were removed to Girard College, a boarding school for orphan boys created by a bequest in his will. This is "the little Catholic churchyard in the heart of the city" referred to in Longfellow's poem "Evangeline." The poem is based on the story of the Acadians, who were exiled from Nova Scotia by the British as punishment for their loyalty to France during the

French and Indian War (1754–63). Hundreds of Acadians came to Philadelphia. Part of Longfellow's poem reads:

> *Side by side, in their nameless graves, the lovers are sleeping.*
> *Under the humble walls of the little Catholic graveyard,*
> *In the heart of the city, they lie, unknown and unnoticed.*

⑩ Across from the church is the **birthplace of Joseph Jefferson (10)** (*600 Spruce, at the southwest corner of Sixth and Spruce Streets*), the greatest American comic actor of the 19th century. (Not open to the public.)

Jefferson was born in Philadelphia of a family associated with the Chestnut Street Theatre. He often played the Walnut Street Theatre, which still stands. Jefferson served as the second president of the prestigious Players Club in New York, following Marylander Edwin Booth. Jefferson's daughter was a friend of Asia Booth, sister of Lincoln assassin John Wilkes Booth, and she was entrusted with the Booth family papers on the Lincoln assassination.

Walk west on Spruce Street, passing No. 614, a Georgian-style, three-story brick house built between 1804 and 1805 for Catherine Howell by James Pancoast, a lumber merchant.

⑪ In the next block of Spruce is the former **home of Nicholas Biddle (11)** (*715 Spruce Street*), scholar, writer, orator and banker who was prominent in Philadelphia from the 1820s to the 1840s. (Not open to the public.)

Biddle was editor of *The Port Folio* and served as director and later president of the Second Bank of the United States. His Federal-period house on Spruce Street was built for wealthy merchant Whitten Evans in 1821 and became Biddle's home about 1830. During his time there, he was involved in a confrontation with President Andrew Jackson over the fate of the Second Bank. Jackson challenged the constitutionality of a national bank and its monopolistic influence on the national economy, and vetoed the bank's charter. So Biddle created a new institution, the United States Bank of Pennsylvania, but it failed. He resigned and went to live on his country estate in Andalusia, near Bristol, Bucks County. The house on Spruce Street, however, remained in the Biddle family for many years. It was later used by the American Catholic Historical Society.

Looking from his home on Washington Square, writer Christopher Morley could see the rear of the mansion and its delightful gardens. Though born in 1890, long after Nicholas Biddle's death in 1844, Morley also could see the impact that such families as the Biddles had on the city. He once described Philadelphia as a "large town at the confluence of the Biddle and Drexel families . . . surrounded by cricket teams, fox hunters, beagle packs, and the Pennsylvania railroad."

⓬ Continue west on Spruce Street to Eighth Street and turn right for the next stop: the Greek Orthodox **Church of St. George (12)** (*256 South Eighth Street*), a superb Greek Revival building designed by John Haviland and erected in 1822 as St. Andrew's Episcopal Church. (Orthros begins at 8:30 a.m. and the Divine Liturgy or Eucharist at 10 a.m. on Sunday. Call ahead to arrange tours.)

St. Andrew's was Haviland's church and his favorite building. The architect based his design on the Temple of Bacchus at Teos, Greece. Six massive, white marble Ionic columns support the entablature, and behind them is a magnificent entrance door. Haviland is buried in a crypt beneath the church. The rectory next door was built in 1840.

⓭ Now walk west on Locust to the **Musical Fund Hall (13)** (*800 block of Locust Street near Eighth Street*), a former concert hall that once played an important role in the cultural and political life of the city. It was later converted into a condominium complex, though signs of its former glory are still evident, such as the lyre on the pediment and the decorative facade. (Not open to the public.)

Originally an uncompleted church, the building was remodeled by several architects: William Strickland in 1824, Napoleon Le Brun in 1847 and Addison Hutton in 1891. The idea for building a hall for public concerts came from the Musical Fund Society, which was founded in 1820 by a group of music lovers, who attended small, private performances in each other's homes. The group included painter Thomas Sully and Francis Drexel, also a painter and founder of the Drexel Company. The society was incorporated in 1823 for "the cultivation of skill and diffusion of taste in music and the relief of [needy] musicians and their families."

The Musical Fund Hall attracted the best musicians and entertainers, as well as the cream of Philadelphia society, from its opening in 1824 until 1857, when the Academy of Music opened on Broad Street. Such singers as Jenny Lind, the "Swedish Nightingale," and Adelina Patti, a famous coloratura of her day, performed here. Many great writers also lectured here: Charles Dickens, Ralph Waldo Emerson, William Makepeace Thackeray and Arthur Conan Doyle, author of the Sherlock Holmes stories.

The hall was the site of the first Republican National Convention in 1856, when John C. Frémont was nominated for president. Not ready to support abolitionist Republicans, the city wound up giving a majority of its votes to Pennsylvanian James Buchanan, the Democrats' nominee, who won the White House. After the music hall's long, colorful history, an effort was made to turn it into a music museum. That failed. The Musical Fund Hall was sold in the 1950s and became the warehouse of a cigar manufacturer for a time before its present incarnation as a condominium complex.

14 Head north on Eighth Street to the **Reynolds-Morris House (14)** (*225 South Eighth Street*), a distinguished-looking brick home built by John Reynolds in 1786–87. (Not open to the public.)

Reynolds sold the house to Luke Wistar Morris, whose father was Capt. Samuel Morris of Germantown, a member of the First City Troop that fought in the Revolutionary War. The home stayed in the Morris family until World War II, when it was purchased by an advertising agency, N.W. Ayer & Sons, which used it as a guest house for important visitors. Now a luxury boutique hotel, the house still stands out, with its Flemish bond brick design with alternating black headers and red stretchers. Note the exquisite doorway, with fluted pilasters and beautiful fanlight. Before leaving, take a look at the garden, with its boxwoods and trees, enclosed by a wrought-iron fence.

15 Walk north on Eighth Street to Walnut Street and turn left for the **Walnut Street Theatre (15)** (*Ninth and Walnut Streets*), the oldest English-speaking theater in continuous use in the United States. (Open year-round for dramatic plays, musicals and comedies.)

The theater was designed by John Haviland and opened in 1809, as the New Circus. It was renamed the Olympic after a stage was added in 1811. The first play was performed on New Year's Day, 1812.

The theater received its present name in 1820—the same year that the Chestnut Street Theatre burned down. Edwin Forrest made both his debut and final appearance here. Others who appeared on the Walnut's stage included Edmund Kean, Otis Skinner, Edwin Booth, George Arliss and John and Ethel Barrymore. After the Theatre Royal in London (built 1809–12), the 1,052-seat Walnut Street Theatre is the oldest playhouse in the English-speaking world.

Walnut Street
Theatre

16 Head south on Ninth to **Bonaparte House (16)** (*260 South Ninth Street*), once the home of Joseph Bonaparte, elder brother of Napoleon and ex-king of Naples (1806–08) and Spain (1808–13). (Not open to the public.)

After Napoleon was defeated at the Battle of Waterloo, Joseph Bonaparte arrived in the United States in 1815. He stopped in Philadelphia on his way to Washington, where he planned to visit President James Madison. But the administration discouraged the visit and Bonaparte located in Philadelphia, with the help of Stephen Girard, a banker and fellow French emigrant. He lived in the Ninth Street house until moving to an estate in Point Breeze on the Delaware River near Bordentown, New Jersey. The house has since been divided into apartments.

17 Walk farther south on Ninth to Spruce Street, turn left and continue to **Mikveh Israel Cemetery (17)** (*Spruce and Darien Streets*). This brick-walled burial ground of Sephardic Jews dates back to 1738 and is the oldest Jewish historic site in Philadelphia. (Guides are available during the summer, from 10 a.m. to 3 p.m. Tuesday through Friday and on Sunday. From September to June, make visiting arrangements with the Mikveh Israel Synagogue office, 44 North Fourth Street. Call 215-922-5446.)

Nathan Levy, a Jewish merchant whose ship, the *Myrtilla*, brought the Liberty Bell to America, received this land from the royal proprietor of Pennsylvania, Thomas Penn, son of William Penn, who wanted his Holy Experiment to embrace all faiths. Levy set aside the land as a family burial ground. It later was used by the Jewish community. Among those buried here is patriot Haym Salomon, a Polish Jew who joined Robert Morris in raising money to finance the Revolutionary War.

Also buried here is Rebecca Gratz, who was the inspiration for Sir Walter Scott's heroine Rebecca in the classic novel *Ivanhoe*. Rebecca, whose family was commercially, socially and politically prominent, had fallen in love with a Christian, Samuel Ewing. A young and beautiful woman who was painted by Thomas Sully, she would not marry outside of her Jewish faith. She devoted her life instead to establishing homes for orphans and unwed mothers. Her story was related to Scott by Washington Irving, who had been engaged to a friend of Rebecca's. (More on this in Walk 2, Stop 14.)

Others buried in the cemetery include Revolutionary War soldiers Benjamin Nones, who served as an officer under Washington; Philip Moses Russel, a surgeon's mate at Valley Forge during the winter of 1777–78; and British deserters who were publicly shot against the brick wall, then placed in an unmarked grave.

18 Farther west on Spruce is the house of **Sarah Josepha Hale (18)**, one of the first successful women magazine editors (*922 Spruce Street*). She was renowned as the editor of *Godey's Lady's Book*, a locally produced women's magazine. (Not open to the public.)

Hale moved to Philadelphia in 1841 and by 1860 her magazine had 150,000 subscribers. She lived in this house from 1859 to 1861. Sarah Hale lobbied Congress and the president to establish a national Thanksgiving Day—and got her wish after the Battle of Gettysburg, when President Lincoln set aside a national day of observance. Hale is probably best known for her poem "Mary Had a Little Lamb," a favorite of children. Her former home is now two private residences.

19 At Eighth and Spruce Streets is **Pennsylvania Hospital (19)**, the oldest hospital in the United States. It contains the nation's first medical library and surgical amphitheater. (Guided tours can be

Pennsylvania
Hospital

arranged 48 hours in advance, 10 a.m. to 1 p.m. Monday through Friday. Call 215-829-5434. Free.)

The hospital was founded in 1751 by Benjamin Franklin, Dr. Thomas Bond and other public-minded citizens interested in establishing a community hospital to improve care for the poor. The Pennsylvania Assembly offered to put up 2,000 pounds if the proponents could match that amount. Franklin had no trouble raising the money and the work got underway. Three physicians, Thomas and Phineas Bond and Lloyd Zachery, offered their services free for three years.

Walk past the modern buildings on Spruce Street, then south on Eighth Street toward Pine Street to get a better view of the older part of the hospital. The east wing nearest to Eighth Street was built in 1755, the west wing in 1796, and the Center House in 1804. The marble pilasters of the Center House stand out against the red brick. On the tour, you will see the Historical Library, which houses the oldest collection of medical books in the country. The hospital also has a portrait gallery and displays of early medical instruments.

On the lawn is a lead statue of William Penn by an unknown artist. It was spotted by Benjamin Franklin in England in 1775, when he served as an agent for Pennsylvania and Massachusetts. The statue graced the London grounds of a Franklin friend, Lord Le Despencer, postmaster general of England. Later John Penn, grandson of William Penn, purchased it in a London junk shop and gave it to the hospital. Legend has it that Penn steps down from his pedestal at midnight on New Year's Eve to take a turn around the grounds.

20 Before leaving the hospital grounds, take a look at the **Treaty Elm (20)** (*Eighth and Pine Streets*). The tree is a direct descendant of the Great Elm of Kensington, under which William Penn concluded his treaty of perpetual friendship with the local Native Americans. The original tree was destroyed in a storm in 1810. Part of the root was given to the hospital and another elm grew from it. That tree was cut down in 1841, when Clinton Street was opened. But cuttings were kept, and one of those has grown into the tree just inside the Eighth Street gate.

21 Head east on Pine Street to our last stop, **Mother Bethel African Methodist Episcopal Church (21)** (*419 South Sixth Street*). This historic church was founded in 1787 by Bishop Richard Allen after he and fellow African Americans left nearby St. George's Methodist Church because of the segregated worship there. Mother Bethel occupies land that has been owned by blacks longer than any other in America. (Museum and guided tours open 10 a.m. to 3 p.m. Tuesday through Saturday. Last tour at 2 p.m. Free will offering accepted.)

Here, in a basement museum, are the simple belongings of Allen, a man of faith and courage who emerged from slavery in 1777 to start a church and fight for civil rights. His Bible rests in a small display case, its cover and pages dog-eared and brittle from age and constant use. Nearby is the large pine pulpit that Allen made by hand and his tapestry-covered stools, showing wear from knees bent there in prayer. The museum is filled with lithographs, rare documents, photographs and church relics, such as handsome Windsor chairs and the "mourner's bench," a long, wooden pew reserved for "sinful family members" who became the focus of preaching.

Richard Allen probably was born at Cliveden, a mansion in Philadelphia's Germantown section, where he was a slave to Quaker lawyer Benjamin Chew, chief justice of Pennsylvania from 1774 to 1777. Allen, his parents and three other children later were sold to a man in Dover, Delaware. But Allen was not content to remain in servitude. After a religious conversion at 17, he and his brother

Mother
Bethel African
Methodist
Episcopal
Church

raised $2,000 in Continental money to buy their freedom, and Allen returned to Philadelphia.

He joined the white congregation of St. George's on Fourth Street. He was licensed to preach in 1784 and was permitted to hold 5 a.m. services at St. George's. But as attendance there grew in 1787, white church members became hostile, and some black parishioners were asked to move to another part of the church during a prayer service. Allen led black parishioners from St. George's and later purchased a parcel of land on which a church was erected. The first building was an abandoned blacksmith shop that was hauled to the location and converted.

Allen was viewed by city leaders as a prominent minister in the black community, and in 1793, during the yellow fever epidemic, he helped lead efforts to care for the sick and bury the dead. He also organized a black militia during the War of 1812 to repel any British

Mother Bethel African Methodist Episcopal Church

invasion. Several muskets used by the militia, now fragile from age, are part of the museum exhibit.

The African Methodist Episcopal Church officially was formed in 1816, and Allen became its first bishop. The present church building, the fourth at the site, was completed in 1890. It is in the Romanesque Revival style, with a square corner tower, beautiful woodwork and stained-glass windows. Allen is interred in the church's crypt, along with his wife and another bishop, Morris Brown.

Walking north on Sixth Street to Walnut will return you to Washington Square, our starting point and now a good spot to relax.

Around City Hall

Around City Hall

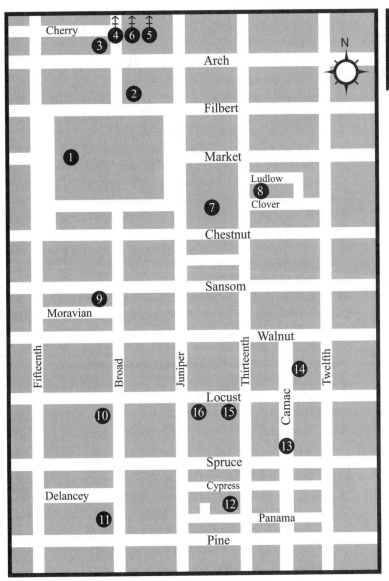

Cherry

Arch

Filbert

Market

Ludlow

Clover

Chestnut

Sansom

Moravian

Walnut

Fifteenth

Broad

Juniper

Thirteenth

Twelfth

Camac

Locust

Spruce

Cypress

Delancey

Panama

Pine

N

USEFUL INFORMATION

As you might guess, with so many offices in the area, restaurants and food courts are numerous and varied. A selection: Chris' Jazz Café-Bar, 1421 Sansom Street, featuring live music; Ruth's Chris Steak House, 18th and Market Streets; Oyster House, 1516 Sansom Street; and the Food Court at the Shops at Liberty Place, 1625 Chestnut Street, between the One Liberty and Two Liberty office towers.

Parking is available at lots and garages near City Hall on Broad Street, Market Street and on several intersecting streets. Numerous metered parking spaces also are available.

If you're making your way on public transportation, you have several choices. The city's transit system, SEPTA, crisscrosses the area. The Broad Street Subway runs north and south, and the Market-Frankford Line runs east and west—both passing beneath City Hall. The PATCO High Speedline also runs underground, with stops at Eighth and Market Streets and along Locust Street, with stations between Ninth and 10th, 12th and 13th, and 15th and 16th Streets. SEPTA buses also run on Broad, Market and Chestnut Streets.

Introduction

City Hall was once the tallest building in Philadelphia, rising 547 feet above street level. And it remained the tallest for a century—not out of adherence to law, but out of respect for tradition. But tradition eventually gave way to Philadelphia's ongoing transformation from an industrial city to a center for service industries. Developers proposed two office towers in 1984 that would break the unwritten height rule. After much debate and soul-searching, city officials relented: City Hall was topped by One Liberty Place in 1987, 100 years after the tower of the massive municipal building had been completed. The public outcry, though, spoke volumes about Philadelphia. It was, and is, a place that respects its history and traditions.

City Hall sits on Centre Square, the focus of William Penn's original plan for five public squares. Long before construction of the building got underway, this was the site of the engine house of Philadelphia's first municipal water works. In the early 1800s, water from the Schuylkill was pumped to a reservoir on high ground, then carried by gravity to the pumping station at the square. An 1812 watercolor by Pavel Petrovich Svinin shows the engine house and a fountain with the *Nymph of the Schuylkill* sculpture by William Rush.

After the Civil War, as more businesses, hotels and private residences located west of Broad Street, pressure grew to move the municipal government to Centre Square, also known as Penn Square. By 1872, work had begun on the new City Hall, and by the 1880s, the building was largely completed, though the finishing touches would not be made until 1901.

Standing at this lavishly embellished building, which has been called a Victorian wedding cake of French Empire and Renaissance styles, you're in the heart of Center City, surrounded by historic buildings, museums and skyscrapers. Here, past and present mingle in a way that makes this walk a pure delight.

The Tour

❶ Let's start with a more detailed look at **City Hall (1)** (*Broad and Market Streets*), the largest in the nation. (Tours are given Monday through Friday. The tower offers a panoramic view of the city. Timed tickets are available in Room 121 on the first floor or in the Tower Exhibit Room on the 9th floor, which is accessible via the northeast corner elevator. Elevators for the tower leave every 15 minutes between 9:30 a.m. and 4:15 p.m. Monday through Friday. A guided tour of the interior of City Hall takes about an hour and includes visits to the Mayor's Reception Room, Conversation Hall and other areas. The tour leaves Room 121 at 12:30 p.m. For details, call 267-514-4757.)

Architect John McArthur Jr. designed this colossal, mansarded building, with help from Thomas U. Walter, architect of the dome and the House and Senate wings of the U.S. Capitol in Washington, D.C. The cornerstone was laid on July 4, 1874. As the city prepared for the Centennial Exhibition of 1876, James D. McCabe, who chronicled the celebration, described Philadelphia's then-new municipal project, with all its modern features.

"It is designed in the spirit of French art, admirable in its ornamentation, while the whole effect is one of massive dignity, worthy of us and our posterity," he wrote. "The entire structure will contain

City Hall

520 rooms, giving ample, convenient and stately provision for all the departments of the city government, including heat, light and ventilation, and the whole is to be absolutely fire-proof and indestructible. The several stories will be reached by four large elevators, placed at the intersections of the leading corridors." The building went up slowly, rising above an interior courtyard, which was accessible to the public through monumental arched portals on all four sides. Workers eventually created more than 600 rooms from 14½ acres of floor space.

The most recognizable feature of City Hall—the icing on the Victorian wedding cake—was Alexander Milne Calder's 36-foot, 8-inch bronze statue of William Penn holding the charter of Pennsylvania, perched atop the massive tower. It is still the largest single piece of sculpture on any building in the world. The statue was displayed in City Hall courtyard for two years before being raised to the top of the tower in 1894. The figure's vital statistics: The hat is 9 feet in diameter and 23 feet in circumference. The face is 3 feet, 3 inches from hat brim to chin; each of the eyes is one foot wide; the nose is 18 inches long. The coat cuffs are 3 feet long; the arms, 12 feet, 6 inches long; the legs are 10 feet from ankle to knee; and the feet are 5 feet, 4 inches long. (A smaller copy of the 27-ton statue can be seen at Welcome Park, visited in Walk 1.)

Calder, grandfather of modern sculptor Alexander Calder of mobile fame, spent decades working on the plaster models for hundreds of other statues that would adorn the building. Some figures represented the seasons and arts, others the continents and science. Allegorical figures, masks and heads also were added. Skilled workmen chipped away at granite, using Calder's designs as their guide.

In the end, the building—with its many statues, unique tower and interpretation of French Renaissance grandeur—was seen by critics as bulky and craggy-looking, even grotesque and pretentious. Yet City Hall withstood the criticisms and efforts to raze it. Indeed, it has been cleaned, dramatically illuminated for night viewing, and now seems ready for long service.

Stroll through the courtyard. In spring, the gardens are lush with tulips and hyacinths. And over the winter holidays, a large Christmas village of vendors spreads out in the courtyard and around the building. Heading inside, climb one flight of stairs at the northeast

City Hall Courtyard

corner of the building to the mayor's wonderfully ornate reception room (Room 202) and restored Conversation Hall (Room 201). The abundant use of marble, carved wood, mahogany paneling and gold-leaf ceilings gives visitors a sense that they have entered a Second Empire salon in Paris. The Pennsylvania Supreme Court and City Council Chambers also are worthy of note before you head to the top of the nation's tallest masonry-bearing building. Imagine: This huge structure is held up without steel supports. From the observation deck beneath the William Penn statue, on a clear day visitors get a magnificent view for two dozen miles or more.

❷ Leaving from the northeast corner of City Hall, walk north across the street to the **Masonic Temple (2)** (*1 North Broad Street*), one of the most ornate and architecturally striking buildings in the city. (Open 9 a.m. to 5 p.m. Tuesday through Saturday. Admission for guided tour $15 for adults; students and seniors $10; and children 12 and under $5. Library and museum only $7.)

Architect James H. Windrim, a Mason, designed the building in the Norman style—and the result, said Philadelphia historian Thompson Westcott, was the finest Masonic structure in the world. This architectural jewel, with its spires and turrets, was begun in 1863 and cost more than $1.6 million. Some 10,000 Masons watched

Masonic Temple

on June 24, 1868, as the trowel used by Brother George Washington to set the cornerstone of the U.S. Capitol was used in the laying of the cornerstone of the new Masonic Temple. J. S. Ingram, who wrote a book, *The Centennial Exposition*, about the 100th anniversary celebration in Philadelphia, said the temple "is built of granite, dressed at the quarry, and brought to the temple ready to be raised at once on its place; so that what was said of Solomon's temple may be said with almost equal truth of this: 'There was neither hammer nor ax nor any tool of iron heard in the house while it was [in] building'" (I Kings 6:7).

Freemasonry, some historians say, started in the 10th century B.C., during the construction of King Solomon's temple. Records clearly show its existence in 926 A.D. in England. The fraternal organization was made up of stoneworkers who traveled throughout Europe using the skills and secrets of their craft. The Free and Accepted Masons grew in numbers over the years, with people in the building trades and other honorary members. The first Masonic lodge in America was established on June 24, 1732, at the Tun Tavern in Philadelphia. The first Masonic building in America was dedicated in 1755 at a location near Second and Walnut Streets. The organization had come a long way by the time a new Masonic temple was finished on Broad Street and celebrated on September 26, 1873, with a parade of 13,000 Masons.

The interior is a wonder to behold. Walk into a Doric grand foyer, then view seven richly adorned lodge halls, representing the Egyptian, Ionic, Corinthian, Oriental, Italian Renaissance, Gothic and Norman styles. Egyptian Hall is breathtaking. The detail and mystic symbols are so accurate that scholars come here to study them. Wherever you walk, there are awe-inspiring marvels—polished marble, oil paintings, statuary and richly carved oak. The temple also contains a library with tens of thousands of volumes and a museum with letters of Washington, Lafayette, Benjamin Franklin and Andrew Jackson.

The museum's most priceless item is Brother Washington's Masonic apron, which was embroidered by Madame Lafayette. Her husband, Brother the Marquis de Lafayette, presented the apron to Washington in August 1784 at Mount Vernon.

❸ Now walk north on Broad Street to **The Pennsylvania Academy of the Fine Arts (3)** (*118 North Broad Street*), America's first true art museum and repository for many historic and contempo-

The Pennsylvania Academy of the Fine Arts

rary masterpieces. (Open 10 a.m. to 5 p.m. Tuesday through Friday, 11 a.m. to 5 p.m. Saturday and Sunday. Adults $15; college students and seniors over 60, $12; youths 13 to 18, $8; military personnel, federal employees and their families, and children 12 and under admitted for free.)

The academy was founded in 1805 by the voluntary contributions of Philadelphia residents, who sought to improve and refine the public taste for works of art. The principal organizers were 71 civic-minded citizens of Philadelphia, including three artists, Charles Willson Peale, his son Rembrandt Peale, and William Rush. "The object of this association is to promote the cultivation of the Fine Arts in the United States of America, by introducing correct and elegant copies from works of the first masters in sculpture and painting and by thus facilitating the access to such standards, and also by occasionally conferring moderate but honorable premiums and otherwise assisting the studies and exciting the efforts of the artist gradually to unfold, enlighten and invigorate the talents of our countrymen," academy officials wrote in their application for a charter.

This building, the academy's home since 1876, was designed by Philadelphia architects Frank Furness and George Hewitt and was one of the city's attractions during the Centennial Exhibition. It sits on the former site of a Civil War hospital. The exterior has a modified Gothic flavor, with stone, brick, tiles and statues of terra-cotta. The interior is lavish, spacious and colorful. Here are great works of art by Thomas Eakins, Benjamin West, Gilbert Stuart, Charles Willson Peale, Andrew Wyeth, William Rush and Rembrandt Peale.

Eakins established himself as one of the most important artists of the 19th century with the completion in 1875 of *The Gross Clinic*, a painting depicting Dr. Samuel Gross explaining an operation from the surgical theater. Among his other well-known paintings are *Max Schmitt in a Single Scull* (1871), *The Chess Players* (1876) and *Margaret in Skating Costume* (1871). The artist, who lived most of his life at 1729 Mount Vernon Street, taught at the academy, where he dramatically changed the curriculum. His devotion to drawing the male and female anatomy—a subject he had studied at Jefferson Medical Academy—brought on a collision with the mores of the day.

➍ Three blocks further north on Broad Street is the former **Inquirer–Daily News Building (4)** (*400 North Broad Street*), an 18-story landmark that was home to *The Philadelphia Inquirer* and its sister newspaper, *The Philadelphia Daily News*. The building was sold in 2011, expected to become the new Philadelphia Police headquarters. The newspapers relocated in 2012 to the third floor of the former Strawbridge and Clothier building at 8th and Market Streets.

Construction of the Broad Street building began in July 1923 and was completed two years later at a cost of $10 million. Designed by Rankin, Kellogg and Crane Architects, this Beaux Arts gem is topped by a four-story clock tower and bronze dome. The classical ornamentation of the building includes columns, pilasters, urns and relief decorations. The first issue of the *Inquirer* came off the presses here on July 13, 1925. At the time, the building was touted as the most modern newspaper plant in the world.

➎ Heading north on Broad Street, a few steps away, you will come to Noble Street, where you can explore Philadelphia's new **Rail Park (5)** (*Broad and Noble Streets*), a free elevated park and recreational pathway that stretches a quarter mile along a section of the old Reading Railroad. The park, which opened in 2018, also has other entrances at 13th and Noble Streets and on Callowhill Street between 11th and 12th Streets. It is expected to eventually extend through ten neighborhoods. Visitors can look forward to plants, trees, plentiful seating and public art.

6 Further north is the **Philadelphia Opera House (6)** (*858 North Broad Street*), now known as the **Met Philadelphia**, a historic opera house built by impresario Oscar Hammerstein in 1908 and now a mixed-use concert venue. It was an opera house through 1934, when it took on different functions as a movie theater, ballroom, sports venue and church. The building was renovated and reopened in 2018 with a concert by rock and folk star Bob Dylan. It's also currently home to a church.

7 Head south on Broad Street, passing the **Arch Street Methodist Church** (*Arch and Broad Streets*), a stately Gothic edifice built of marble between 1868 and 1873. Walk past the Masonic Temple to Market Street. Just east of City Hall is **Macy's**, housed in the former **John Wanamaker department store (7)** (*Market Street between Juniper and 13th Streets*). Wanamaker's was the city's landmark store. (Open 10 a.m. to 8 p.m. Monday through Saturday and 11 a.m. to 7 p.m. on Sunday.)

John Wanamaker began a clothing store in 1861 and became one of the nation's most successful business executives. In 1902, he built the store near City Hall, designed by Daniel H. Burham of Chicago. A brass plate in the floor of the nine-story grand court commemorates a visit by President William Howard Taft on December 30, 1911, when he dedicated the building.

A mammoth pipe organ—the largest in the world—and a 2,500-pound bronze eagle are the most popular attractions in the grand court. Both had been made for the St. Louis Exposition of 1904. The 30,000-pipe organ is played daily and is part of a holiday sound-and-light show. The eagle is a favorite rendezvous point for shoppers. "Meet me at the eagle" became a common Philadelphia expression. Wanamaker saw *himself* in that eagle. He once said that "anyone can be a shopkeeper, but a merchant is as much different as . . . a Rocky Mountain eagle [is] from a mouse."

8 Leave Macy's on the Chestnut Street side, then walk east to 13th Street and north to **St. John the Evangelist Roman Catholic Church (8)** (*21 South 13th Street near Chestnut Street*), the second Cath-

St. John
the Evangelist
Roman Catholic
Church

olic cathedral in the city. (Masses at 7:45 a.m., 12:05 p.m., 1:05 p.m. and 5:15 p.m. weekdays; 7:45 a.m., 12:05 p.m. and 5:15 p.m. Saturday; and 8:30 a.m., 10:30 a.m., 12:30 p.m. and 6 p.m. on Sunday. For more information on other services in the main sanctuary and in the lower church meeting area, call 215-563-4145.)

The church was built in 1832 but was not used as a cathedral until 1838. The small cemetery plot next to the church holds the remains of Madame Anna Maria Huarte de Iturbide, the empress who became a Philadelphian. She was the widow of Gen. Augustin de Iturbide, who was chosen emperor of Mexico on May 19, 1822, by the deputies of the Mexican Congress. His reign was brief. Gen. Santa Ana forced his abdication on March 19, 1823. The Iturbide family was exiled to Italy, but the emperor returned in May 1823 to rally his forces. He was captured and executed on July 19, 1824. Before his death, he declared, "I am no traitor! Such a stain will never attach to my children or to their descendants."

His wife, Anna Maria Huarte, and their children eventually came to Philadelphia, where they lived near Spruce and 13th Streets and later at 226 South Broad Street. The former empress died here in 1861 at 79. A son, Augustin, and daughter, Sabrina, are interred with her in vault No. 9, as well as two other children whose remains were brought here from Mexico in 1849 for reburial.

9 Head west on Chestnut Street to Broad, turn left and walk to the **Union League (9)** (*Broad and Sansom Streets*), a private social club whose members rallied to the cause of the Union during the Civil War. Members still meet in this elegant, brownstone, French Renaissance building erected in 1865. (The Heritage Center of the Union League is open to the public 3 to 6 p.m. Tuesday and

Union League

Thursday and 1 to 4 p.m. on the second Saturday of every month to view exhibits and conduct research. For more information, call 215-587-6455.)

The Union League was conceived in November 1862 during a meeting between George Boker, a brilliant dramatist, and Judge John Innes Clark Hare, a distinguished jurist. The two had become increasingly concerned about pro-Southern sympathy in the city. No strong Union organization had been formed to counter the threat. "In this miserable condition of public affairs, we fell into a conversation that was little more than a comparison of sorrows," Boker later recalled. "'Is there no remedy for this state of affairs?' Judge Hare asked me. 'Can we not, at least, withdraw from all social relations with disloyal men and set up a society of our own?'"

The first meeting of patriotic gentlemen took place on November 15, 1862, at 226 South Fourth Street, home of Benjamin Gerhard. Gradually, from modest beginnings, the Union League grew. "The condition of membership shall be unqualified loyalty to the government of the United States, and unwavering support of its efforts for the suppression of the Rebellion," read the new group's articles of association. "The primary object of the Association shall be to discountenance and rebuke by moral and social inference all disloyalty to the Federal government, and to that end the Association will use every proper means in public and private." The Union League's first clubhouse was the Hartman Kuhn mansion at 1118 Chestnut Street. By 1865, it had moved into the new Broad Street facility that it still occupies.

The nation's leaders have walked the venerable hallways of this building—presidents and war heroes, such as Ulysses S. Grant, Theodore Roosevelt and Dwight D. Eisenhower. They've chatted about world affairs beneath frescoed ceilings and bright brass chandeliers. And they've supped at banquets and clinked glasses amid sculptures, paintings, marble floors and redwood paneling. Since its opening, when a Philadelphia newspaper compared the building to a "thoroughly well-dressed woman," the Union League has witnessed history and hosted the people who made it.

Members told President Abraham Lincoln about the forthcoming opening of the club's building when he visited Philadelphia in 1864. He promised he would return for the ceremony. Before he could do it, Lincoln was assassinated by John Wilkes Booth in Washington. The country's joy over the end of the Civil War turned to grief, and the league's celebration was never held. Instead of red, white and blue bunting to welcome the President's return, the new building was adorned in black crepe as Lincoln's body lay in state for public viewing at Independence Hall.

Inside the Union League headquarters—now nestled amid taller, more modern structures—is Victorian grandeur: a graceful, sweeping double staircase, oil paintings, sculpture, stained-glass windows, fine furniture and sumptuous dining rooms. In the 20th century, membership came to represent the epitome of social class for Philadelphia gentlemen. Women were not allowed to join them as members until 1986, when the Union League voted 950 to 426 to end its ban on female membership.

10 Moving further south on Broad Street—this stretch is called the Avenue of the Arts—we arrive at the **Academy of Music (10)** (*Broad and Locust Streets*), the oldest concert hall and opera house in the country. This building has provided a stage for some of the nation's best-known artists and musicians since 1857. The Academy of Music has been home to the Philadelphia Orchestra since the orchestra's creation in 1900, and also hosts the Pennsylvania Ballet. (For information on tours, call 215-790-5886.)

The concert hall was designed by architect Napoleon Le Brun, who based the lavish interior on the La Scala opera house in Milan. Construction began in 1855 and the academy opened with a ball on January 26, 1857. Since then, audiences have taken in performances by great singers, such as Adelina Patti, and by renowned conductors and composers, including Tchaikovsky.

The future King Edward VII came here in 1860, when he was Prince of Wales, and sat in a balcony box, now called the Prince of Wales Box. Edward reportedly was smitten with the young Adelina Patti, who was performing here when she was about 16. In 1871, the academy hosted a spectacular ball honoring the Grand Duke Alexis of Russia, son of Czar Alexander II.

The large seating capacity also made it a good location for a political convention. In 1872, Ulysses S. Grant was nominated here. And Presidents Woodrow Wilson, William McKinley and Grover Cleveland addressed audiences here.

The academy's noble facade—fine-pressed red brick exterior, brownstone trimmings and gas lamps—still conjures up images of the Victorian era, when horse-drawn carriages pulled up on Broad Street to discharge formally attired passengers for an evening of music. Imagine the women in long, full dresses and men in top hats.

Academy of Music

Inside, the neo-Baroque surroundings are plush, from the hall's elaborate painting motifs and carvings to the stunning crystal chandelier, which is lowered periodically for cleaning. The old-world grandeur stands in contrast to the modern elegance of the nearby Kimmel Center for the Performing Arts (farther south on Broad Street at Spruce Street). Gaze upward at the distinctive glass canopy of the center, designed by Rafael Vinoly, and, through it, view Beaux Arts and late-Victorian commercial buildings.

11 Walk south on Broad Street to Dorrance Hamilton Hall, the landmark building of **The University of the Arts (11)** (*Broad and Pine Streets*), a Greek Revival building designed by architect John Haviland and once the site of the Philadelphia Asylum for the Deaf and Dumb. (Check for times of student exhibits.)

David G. Seixas, a Philadelphia crockery and tin merchant, introduced a system of manual communication and founded the Institute for the Deaf and Dumb in 1820. The building on Broad Street was constructed between 1824 and 1825. After a dispute between Seixas and members of his board, he was ousted and the institution was given a new name—the Philadelphia Asylum for the Deaf and Dumb.

Now, as the University of the Arts, the building offers arts education, with undergraduate and graduate degree programs in design, fine arts, crafts, media arts, dance, music, theater, writing for film and television, multimedia and communication. Just past the four massive columns, atop a flight of steps, are state-of-the-art laboratories and studios.

⓬ Head east on Pine Street for **St. Luke and the Epiphany (12)** (*330 South 13th Street*), a magnificent Greek Revival church erected between 1839 and 1841. (Holy Eucharist at 9 a.m. and 11 a.m. Sundays, from Labor Day through June; 10 a.m. Sundays from July through Labor Day; also 6:30 p.m. Tuesdays, prayer and Holy Eucharist. Call ahead for tours: 215-732-1918.)

St. Luke and the Epiphany resulted from the union in 1898 of two Episcopal churches—St. Luke's Church and the Church of the Epiphany. The building has cast-iron Corinthian columns, large entrance doors and beautiful stained-glass windows bearing images of the apostle. A side chapel, designed later by architect Frank Furness, has a Gothic Revival flair that is almost flamboyant.

The church was used as a model for St. Paul's Church in Richmond, Virginia, where Confederate President Jefferson Davis was attending a service in 1865 when he learned of the surrender of his forces under Gen. Robert E. Lee at Appomattox.

⓭ Walk north on 13th Street, turn right on Spruce, then left on South Camac to see an unusual **street of little clubs (13)** (*200 block of South Camac Street*).

Historians Nathaniel Burt and Wallace E. Davies have remarked, in *Philadelphia: A 300-Year History*, on what a "clubby" place Philadelphia is—what they see as evidence of "the cohesive group consciousness, the basically conformist atmosphere that pervaded the city" in the late 19th and early 20th century. Social clubs, like the Union League and the Philadelphia Club; literary and art clubs (the Franklin Inn, Penn Club, Sketch Club); cricket clubs (Philadelphia, Merion, Germantown); women's clubs (Acorn Club) and clubs for businessmen (the Manufacturers Club) proliferated in the years between the end of the Civil War and the start of the First World War. Vestiges still can be found on South Camac Street.

The **Philadelphia Sketch Club** (*235 South Camac*) is the oldest professional artists' club in the country. It was founded in 1860 by students of The Pennsylvania Academy of the Fine Arts. N. C. Wyeth,

Joseph Pennel, Thomas Eakins and Howard Chandler Christy were members. (For more information, call 215-545-9298.)

The **Charlotte Cushman Club** (formerly on Camac Street) was established about 1907 as a respectable home for actresses on tour. The club's board decided in 1999 to close its doors, saying that it had outlived its original residential and educational purposes. Named after the 19th-century American actress, the club offered other female stage entertainers a place to stay in its half-dozen small rooms. Today, though, visiting actresses stay at hotels or return to New York after a performance.

Club memorabilia, including artifacts, photos and newspaper articles, are exhibited in a display case and in a conference room at Terra Hall of the University of the Arts, 211 South Broad Street.

The **Plastic Club** (*247 South Camac*) is the oldest women's art club in America. Founded in 1897, it offers membership to women painters and sculptors. (Open to the public when an exhibit is being shown. Phone 215-545-9324.)

14 Strolling north on Camac, you come to the **Franklin Inn Club (14)** (*205 South Camac, north of Locust Street*), a private literary club founded in 1902 by historical novelist S. Weir Mitchell and his friends. (Not open to the public.)

Members have included such Philadelphia writers as Christopher Morley, Howard Pyle and Joseph Hergesheimer. The club's house is actually two houses, erected in 1795 for Richard Wistar, merchant and member of the board of directors of the Library Company, and Francis Higgins, a weaver. The houses were purchased by the club in 1907 and were renovated in 1999.

15 Now walk south on Camac, then west on Locust to the **Historical Society of Pennsylvania (15)** (*1300 Locust Street*), one of the oldest historical societies in the United States and repository of the largest privately owned collection of manuscripts, books, microfilm and prints covering the history of Pennsylvania and the 12 other original colonies. (Open 12:30 to 5:30 p.m. Tuesday; 12:30 to 8:30 p.m. Wednesday; 12:30 to 5:30 p.m. Thursday; and 10 a.m. to 5:30 p.m. Friday. Admission $8. Students and military members with current identification free. For information, call 215-732-6200.)

The society was founded in 1824, shortly after Lafayette visited the city, reminding Philadelphia of its glorious past. The new organization was first located in Philosophical Hall, later moved to the

Athenaeum, then to the "Picture House" of Pennsylvania Hospital in 1872. It relocated again in 1882 to the spacious mansion of General Robert Patterson at the corner of 13th and Locust Streets, where an assembly hall was added.

The building at 1300 Locust, which has housed the society's collections since 1910, underwent a two-year, $7.6 million renovation and reopened in 1999. The work included restoration of the reading room on the first floor; modernization of reader services, catalog and microfilm areas; installation of environmental equipment for optimal preservation conditions; a new electronic security system; and repair of a portion of the building's exterior.

The historical society's research center has been an important resource for scholars and genealogists, who find original diaries, business records and rare, early American histories not available anywhere else. The center houses more than 21 million books, graphic works and manuscript items.

16 A few steps west on Locust Street bring us to our last stop, the **Library Company of Philadelphia (16)** *(1314 Locust Street)*, the oldest public library in America. This repository contains a half-million printed volumes, 75,000 graphics, 160,000 manuscripts and a small, distinguished collection of early American paintings, portraits and artifacts. (Open 9 a.m. to 4:45 p.m. weekdays. For information, call 215-456-3181. No admission charge.)

In a display window facing Locust Street is the statue of Benjamin Franklin by sculptor Francesco Lazzarini that was once part of the Library Company's building on Fifth Street, south of Chestnut Street. The Library Company was founded in 1731 by Benjamin Franklin and his Junto, a club of influential people who read and discussed political and philosophical matters. Only the library's shareholders could borrow books. Everyone else read them at the library, which moved many times over more than 200 years.

Describing the institution's value to Philadelphia in December 1771, the directors of the Library Company wrote that "about forty Years since, divers public-spirited Inhabitants, desirous to promote the Growth of useful Knowledge, founded a public Library in this City, which from the Encouragement it hath received is now become large & valuable, a Source of Instruction to Individuals and conducive of Reputation to the Public." The membership included 10 signers of the Declaration of Independence.

Statue of
Benjamin
Franklin at
the Library
Company of
Philadelphia

The library, which moved to its present location in 1879, accumulated more than 400,000 volumes, including first editions of Whitman's *Leaves of Grass* and Melville's *Moby-Dick*. But beyond that, it has served as a museum, with the earliest painting of Philadelphia in 1720, a plaster bust of Benjamin Franklin, William Penn's desk and a 1776 copy of Thomas Paine's "Common Sense." While you're here, stop in to see changing exhibits at the Louise Lux-Sions and Harry Sions Gallery.

From here, continue west to Broad Street, then look to the right to find your starting point—City Hall.

Rittenhouse Square: The Good Life

Rittenhouse Square: The Good Life

1. Rittenhouse Square
2. Henry P. McIlhenny House
3. Church of the Holy Trinity
4. Rittenhouse Club
5. Curtis Institute of Music
6. The Barclay
7. Philadelphia Art Alliance
8. St. Mark's Episcopal Church
9. Print Center and Gallery Store
10. Cosmopolitan Club
11. Tenth Presbyterian Church
12. Delancey Place and Plays and Players Theatre
13. Home of Gen. George Gordon Meade
14. Panama Street
15. Rosenbach Museum and Library
16. Home of Pearl S. Buck
17. First Unitarian Church
18. Mütter Museum at the College of Physicians
19. Schuylkill Banks Boardwalk

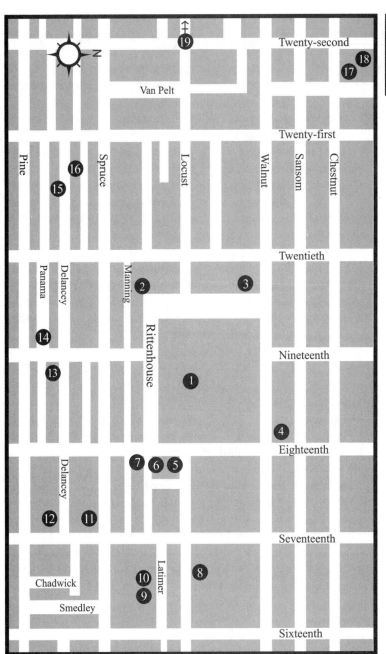

Introduction

Rittenhouse Square has always been known for its old-world charm and elegance. Sitting on a bench here, one can easily imagine a slower-paced time: the sound of creaky carriages and clopping horses' hooves, the sight of neatly attired businessmen in top hats, women with full dresses and parasols, and ornate Victorian mansions of all shapes and sizes.

The graceful Italianate house of railroad tycoon Joseph Harrison Jr. had a prominent spot on 18th Street. The Church of the Holy Trinity, with its Romanesque facade, was set on the northwest corner of the square like a jewel. Nearby was the beautiful St. Mark's Episcopal Church, a Gothic Revival brownstone. And other handsome brownstone buildings across the area provided an air of dignity and class.

Such a lovely setting shows us again why Philadelphia is a walking city—a place that can only fully be discovered on foot.

Originally known as the southwest square in William Penn's plan for the city, the site at 18th and Walnut Streets had once been a field where sheep and cows grazed. It was named in 1825 to honor David Rittenhouse, a veritable Renaissance man whose contributions to Philadelphia and the country are renowned. Rittenhouse was a clock maker, professor of astronomy at the University of Pennsylvania, president of the American Philosophical Society, first director of the United States Mint, and member of the General Assembly and State Constitutional Convention. Over time, the square named for this gifted man took shape, attracting more residents to the area as the city grew westward.

Streets were built on the west and south sides of the square in the 1830s, and the first house facing the square was constructed about 1840. Many grand mansions followed. Rittenhouse Square was becoming one of Philadelphia's exclusive addresses—the place where the city's most wealthy and influential people lived. The entrances to the park, stone railings, pool, fountains and plaza were designed in 1913 by Paul Cret, who helped plan the Benjamin Franklin Parkway. The improvements gave the square the inviting ambience of a Parisian park that drew countless people to relax on its benches, feed the pigeons or take a stroll.

Many well-to-do residents left the city in the 1920s, but pockets of gentility remained. And one of them was Rittenhouse Square— a place still home to leaders of society. By the 1950s, many of the large private houses were gone, either converted to apartments or razed to make way for luxury hotels and apartment buildings. But the charming square—still a green oasis amid attractive buildings— remains one of the most desirable and chic places to live in the city. Art, civic and flower shows are held annually in the park.

One of the square's most attractive features is the fountain, which underwent a $140,000 restoration in 2000. The work—which restored the fountain's original 1913 splendor—brought back a design not seen since the early days of the First World War. The original designer was Paul Cret, head of the architecture department at the University of Pennsylvania and a French citizen.

The fountainhead in the wall represented Neptune, the Roman god of the sea, and its mural depicted Neptune's world—a garden of seaweed populated by salamanders, snails and turtles. Sometime during the First World War, it was torn out. A Fairmount Park commissioner thought it was too frivolous. But the original design was found in the archives of the Athenaeum of Philadelphia, and the restoration was funded by the Friends of Rittenhouse Square.

Today, people still sit beside the pool here or bask in the sun. Children still ogle the Albert Laessle goat, lion and frog. People still feed the pigeons, as they did long ago in a less hurried time.

The Tour

1-**2** Stroll through **Rittenhouse Square (1)** (*18th and Walnut Streets*) to the southwest corner, taking in its old-world charm. Though many of the great Victorian houses around Rittenhouse Square have been torn down, some still remain, including a magnificent townhouse on the southwest corner that once belonged to **Henry P. McIlhenny (2)** (*1914–1916 West Rittenhouse Square*). (Not open to the public.)

McIlhenny was one of Philadelphia's great connoisseurs and an astute, monied patron of the arts. He filled his home with works by

Rittenhouse
Square

Church of the
Holy Trinity

Cézanne, Chardin, Manet, Renoir, Matisse, Ingres and other masters. When he died in 1986, McIlhenny donated his entire collection, including paintings valued at more than $50 million, to the Philadelphia Museum of Art. The mansion was restored and redeveloped in recent years.

❸ On the northwest corner of the square is the **Church of the Holy Trinity (3)** (*Walnut Street and West Rittenhouse Street*), a brownstone designed by John Notman (architect of the Athenaeum) and built between 1857 and 1859. (Episcopal communion service 11 a.m. on Sunday. Tours available. Office hours 9:30 a.m. to 3:30 p.m. Monday through Thursday. Call 215-567-1267.)

The church's rector at the time of its construction was the Rev. Phillips Brooks, who wrote the words to "O Little Town of Bethlehem."

4 At the square's northeast corner is the former **Rittenhouse Club (4)** (*1811 Walnut Street*), once an exclusive private club frequented by novelist Henry James. Following a 1906 visit, James described Philadelphia as a city that was "settled, confirmed and content." The elegant facade was preserved and the building has housed retail shops and residential condominiums.

5 On 18th Street, walk south to the **Curtis Institute of Music (5)** (*1726 Locust Street, at 18th and Locust*), an internationally renowned, tuition-free conservatory of music that occupies an 1893 mansion once owned by banker George W. Childs. (Students typically offer free public recitals at 6 p.m. Monday and 8 p.m. Wednesday and Friday. Tours available 4:30 to 5:30 on Mondays followed by a free student recital at 6 p.m. in the Field Concert Hall.)

The school was founded in 1922 by Mary Louise Curtis Bok, daughter of the founder of Curtis Publishing Company. Among the famous musicians who have studied or taught at Curtis are composers Samuel Barber and Gian Carlo Menotti, soprano Anna Moffo and violinist Efrem Zimbalist, who was music director from 1941 to 1968. He was succeeded by pianist Rudolf Serkin.

Curtis Institute of Music

The Barclay

Don't be surprised to hear pleasant sounds of brass or stringed instruments wafting through the air. The institute also occupies other buildings that were once private homes. Knapp Hall, originally built as a copy of a French townhouse, was the home of wealthy shipbuilder Theodore F. Cramp.

6 Next to the Curtis Institute, on the southeast side of the square, is the 22-story **Barclay (6)** (*237 South 18th Street*), once one of the most fashionable and courtly hotels in the country.

The Barclay was owned by wealthy Philadelphia builder John McShain and known for its old-world charm. It hosted visiting royalty and movie stars and, with its wood paneling and elegant furniture, had a well-heeled quality that fit in with the genteel dowager, Rittenhouse Square. In 1999, the former hotel was converted into condominium apartments.

7 On the southeast side of the square is the **Philadelphia Art Alliance (7)** (*251 South 18th Street*), which sponsors art exhibits and other cultural events. It is housed in the former Samuel Price Wetherill mansion, built in the 1890s. In addition to its gallery shows, the Art Alliance hosts musicals and lectures. In 2018, the alliance became part of the University of the Arts. (Open 11 a.m. to 5 p.m. Tuesday through Friday.)

8 Head east on Locust to **St. Mark's Episcopal Church (8)** (*1600 block of Locust Street*), designed by John Notman and built between 1848 and 1851. With its majestic tower and lovely interior, this English Gothic Revival brownstone is one of the most aesthetically pleasing churches in the area. (Weekdays: 7:30 a.m. Low Mass, 9 a.m. morning prayer, 12:10 p.m. Low Mass and 5:30 p.m. evening prayer. Saturday: 10 a.m. Low Mass and 10:30 a.m. Rosary. Sunday: 8 a.m. Low Mass, 9 a.m. Family Mass, 10 a.m. Christian Formation, September to June, and 11 a.m. Choral High Mass.)

In 1999, for the first time in 123 years, St. Mark's tolled its bells the way they were meant to be rung, a process known as change ringing. Instead of chiming back and forth, the bells were put through a full range of motion, turning in complete circles before returning to their original position. The bells were cast by the same British firm that made the Liberty Bell. They were put back in service after experts spent nearly a year replacing a worn frame and bell mounts with steel fittings.

The church installed four bells in 1876 to commemorate the nation's Centennial and first rang them for Sunday services that June. Residents complained about the noise, and a court issued an injunction against any more calls to worship. The church added four more bells in 1878 and moved all eight bells higher in the tower. Unfortunately, they didn't have enough room to perform as they were designed to. They could chime but not change. The church in the 1980s commissioned a study of the bells, which concluded that the wood frame and fittings should be replaced with steel. Money was raised to install new fittings and lower the bells in the tower. And in 1999 the bells again made a joyous noise.

9 Walk south on 17th Street to Latimer Street, turn left there and walk to the **Print Center (9)** (*1614 Latimer Street*). The center—originally founded in 1915 as the Print Club of Philadelphia—is run by a nonprofit organization of artists and art collectors who have an interest in printmaking and photography as important contemporary art. (Open 11 a.m. to 6 p.m. Tuesday through Saturday. Free.)

Located in a late-19th-century carriage house, the Print Center has exhibits, ongoing educational programs and demonstrations in printmaking and photography. The Gallery Store—opened in 1991— offers for sale the work of more than 100 artists.

10 Next door is the **Cosmopolitan Club (10)** (*1616 Latimer Street*), a private women's club that has art exhibits and lectures for members and their guests. (Not open to the public.)

11 Return to 17th Street and walk south to **Tenth Presbyterian Church (11)** (*17th and Spruce Streets*), a meticulously kept church built between 1850 and 1875. (Free tours available by appointment. Services at 9 a.m., 11 a.m. and 6:30 p.m. on Sunday. Children's Bible school 9 a.m. and 6:30 a.m. Sunday.)

Notice the handsome ironwork in the fence and in the fixtures at the front of the church.

12 Continuing south on 17th brings you to **Delancey Place (12)**, where you will find the historic **Plays and Players Theatre (12)** (*1700 block of Delancey Place*), a 290-seat auditorium with a wonderful view and acoustics. The theater, located on a lovely, tree-lined street of brick townhouses, was once home to the Philadelphia Theatre Company, the city's leading producer of contemporary American plays. Since the Philadelphia Theatre Company relocated to Broad Street in 2007, Plays and Players has been home to a combination of touring shows and local productions.

13 Walk west on Delancey to 19th Street. Look to the left at the one-time **home of Gen. George Gordon Meade (13)** (*1836 Delancey Place at 19th Street*), the Civil War commander who led Union troops to victory at Gettysburg. Meade later became commissioner of Fairmount Park, a post he held until his death in 1872. (Not open to the public.)

The house was given to Meade by the City of Philadelphia, whose residents were thankful for his victory in the crucial 1863 battle. The Meade name can still be read in large letters above the doorway facing on 19th Street. The building now houses apartments.

14 Just south of Meade's house, look to your right for **Panama Street (14)** (*1900 block of Panama Street*), a charming, tree-lined street that has long been the home of musicians, artists and writers.

The 2000 block of Delancey Place

⓯ Follow Delancey west to the **Rosenbach Museum and Library (15)** (*2008–2010 Delancey Place*), two 19th-century townhouses filled with art works, rare books and manuscripts acquired by antique dealers and brothers Philip H. and A.S.W. Rosenbach. (Open 12 to 8 p.m. Tuesday through Thursday, 12 to 5 p.m. Friday and 12 to 6 p.m. Saturday and Sunday. Closed on Monday. Last guided tour at 2:45 p.m. Admission $10, seniors $8, students and children $5, children under 5 free. Tours are included in admission. They are offered on the hour and last 50 minutes.)

Within the walls of this magnificent museum is a vast collection of treasures found nowhere else: the first book printed in what is now the United States (1640); the only known copy of the first book printed in Pennsylvania (1685); the only known first edition of Benjamin Franklin's *Poor Richard's Almanack* (1733); the original manuscript of James Joyce's *Ulysses*; letters of Cortez, Pizarro and De Soto; a first edition of *Don Quixote* and a first edition of *Pilgrim's Progress*. The list of literary gems goes on and on. The museum holds 400,000 rare books, manuscripts and fine and decorative art objects.

The Rosenbach brothers also amassed large collections of art and antique furniture and furnishings. The houses, with high ceilings and attractive, spacious rooms, contain paintings by Sully, Lawrence and Canaletto; drawings by Blake, Fragonard and Daumier; 18th-century English furniture, including Hepplewhite, Chippendale, Sheraton and Adam; and the living room of poet Marianne Moore.

16 Continue west on tree-lined Delancey, passing what was once the home of famed writer **Pearl S. Buck (16)** (*2019 Delancey Place*). (Not open to the public.) The novelist won the Nobel Prize in 1938 for *The Good Earth* and other stories about Chinese life just before the outbreak of World War II.

17 Walking west on Delancey Place, make a right turn onto 21st Street, then a left on Chestnut Street to the **First Unitarian Church (17)** (*Chestnut and Van Pelt Streets*). Established in 1796, it is the oldest church in North America to call itself Unitarian. (Services at 11 a.m. on Sunday. Tours by appointment.)

English scientist and Unitarian minister Joseph Priestly encouraged the founding of the church. The parish house was finished in 1884, and the church was dedicated in 1886. The only church designed by famous Philadelphia architect Frank Furness, it exhibits the congregation's religious philosophy and Furness' special style.

18 Our next-to-last stop is the **Mütter Museum at the College of Physicians (18)** (*19 South 22nd Street*). This is an unusual, if not unique, collection of medical specimens, instruments and lore that may not be appropriate for people with weak stomachs. (Open 10 a.m. to 5 p.m. daily. Admission is $20 for adults, $17 for military service members, $18 for seniors 65 and above, $15 for students and youths 6 to 17; children 5 and under free.)

Where else could you see a plaster cast of the Siamese twins, Chang and Eng Bunker, who died in 1874? Pieces of Albert Einstein's brain? Or a cancerous tumor removed from President Grover Cleveland's jawbone during a secret operation in 1893 on the yacht *Oneida* in the East River of New York?

Named for Dr. Thomas Mütter and established in 1849, the museum contains more than 130 skulls; a 7-foot, 6-inch skeleton; bones shattered by bullets; and hundreds of other anatomical and pathological specimens and organs.

19 Head south on 22nd Street to Locust Street, make a right and follow Locust to the east bank of the Schuylkill River, where you can stroll along the **Schuylkill Banks Boardwalk (19)** (*on the Schuylkill between Locust and South Streets*), a 2,000-foot pathway that allows you to walk, run or cycle over the river while taking in some of Philadelphia's best skyline views. The boardwalk juts out as much as 50 feet from the shore and is 15 feet wide, so there's plenty of room for everybody. It's a fun way to end our walk.

University City and West Philadelphia

University City and West Philadelphia

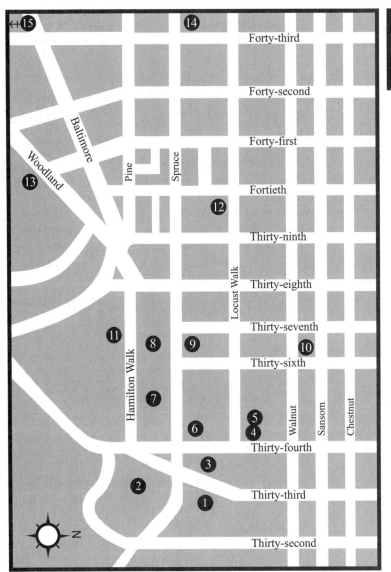

Forty-third

Forty-second

Forty-first

Fortieth

Thirty-ninth

Thirty-eighth

Thirty-seventh

Thirty-sixth

Thirty-fourth

Thirty-third

Thirty-second

Baltimore

Woodland

Pine

Spruce

Locust Walk

Hamilton Walk

Walnut

Sansom

Chestnut

N

> **USEFUL INFORMATION**
>
> Uniersity City has many restaurants with varying prices. Try the White Dog Cafe, 3420 Sansom Street; Zavino, 3200 Chestnut Street; Baby Blues BBQ Philly, 3402 Sansom Street; Han Dynasty, 3711 Market Street; and the New Delhi Indian Restaurant, 4004 Chestnut Street.
>
> Parking garages are located near 34th Street and Civic Center Boulevard. Metered parking also is available.
>
> Getting around is easy. The Route 42 and 21 bus lines run through University City. A SEPTA rail line runs from the Market East Station to the University City Station. In 1999, a SEPTA shuttle bus called LUCY began service through the area. The service links the major cultural and employment centers in University City and operates Monday through Friday, except major holidays.

Introduction

West Philadelphia may not seem compact enough for a walking tour. It covers a vast area, extending more than two miles west of the Schuylkill. But within its boundaries is a small, jewel-like community with a character all its own: University City. Here, the campuses of the University of Pennsylvania, Drexel University and the University of the Sciences in Philadelphia come together. Here, too, is the Institute of Contemporary Art, the Annenberg Center for the Performing Arts, the Arthur Ross Gallery, and the University of Pennsylvania Museum of Archaeology and Anthropology, commonly called the Penn Museum.

This section of the city was part of land bought from the local Native Americans by William Warner in 1677 and used for farming by the early settlers. A permanent bridge was built over the Schuylkill in 1805, which encouraged development of the area. The population quickly increased from several hundred to more than a thousand. By the mid-1800s, well-to-do Philadelphians had built estates and summer homes here. It became a wealthy western suburb and was incorporated into the city in 1854.

By the 1870s, the University of Pennsylvania had moved here from

Ninth and Chestnut Streets—the first classes were held on the new campus in the fall of 1872—and the growth of the area took off. The university purchased many historic Victorian homes, and others were taken over by fraternities. The Quadrangle, with the first dormitory buildings on the Penn campus, went up in the 1890s, giving the school the Gothic look of a European university. At about the same time, the Drexel Institute of Art, Science and Industry—which is today's Drexel University—opened for classes.

The building and improvements across the area mushroomed in the 20th century, surrounding the Gothic structures of the Quad with modern masterpieces of architecture, such as Louis Kahn's Richards Medical Building, completed in 1962. In 1999, the University of Pennsylvania opened a new 238-room hotel—the Inn at Penn—as the centerpiece of Sansom Common, the school's $120 million retail project, bordered by Walnut, Chestnut, 36th and 38th Streets. The inn has architectural details and design features derived from the Arts and Crafts Movement of the early 20th century and is reminiscent of some of the older buildings on the Penn campus.

The colleges give this part of the city its own atmosphere. Indeed, the best time of year to visit University City is when the colleges have classes and students can be seen rushing about.

The Tour

❶ Start on the Penn campus, at a point every student is familiar with: the **statue of "Benjamin Franklin in 1723" (1)** (*33rd Street near Spruce Street*). The work depicts Franklin as a young man arriving in Philadelphia full of hope and ideas. Franklin would go on to found the University of Pennsylvania in 1740, along with numerous other institutions. But in this statue, by R. Tait McKenzie, he's forever young, just starting out life in the city.

❷ Walk south on 33rd Street to the **University of Pennsylvania Museum of Archaeology and Anthropology (commonly called the Penn Museum) (2)** (*33rd and Spruce Streets*), a veritable treasure trove of rare archaeological artifacts that tell the story of ancient and primitive cultures. (Open 10 a.m. to 5 p.m. Tuesday through Sunday; 10 a.m. to 8 p.m. on first Wednesdays. Closed Mondays and holidays. Admission $18 for adults; $16 for seniors 65 and

University of Pennsylvania Museum of Archaeology
and Anthropology

over; $13 for youths 6 to 17 and students with ID; and free for children 5 and under and active-duty military.)

Founded in 1887, the museum is dedicated to the study and understanding of human history and diversity. It is one of the leading archeological museums in the world, with fine collections of objects from ancient Egypt, Persia, Mesopotamia, Greece, China, South America and Middle America. More than a million items—both art and artifacts—have been assembled here from hundreds of expeditions sponsored by the University of Pennsylvania.

The museum was originally located on the top floor of College Hall and opened to the public in 1889. As more artifacts began to accumulate, the museum was relocated in 1890 to the newly erected University Library, designed by architect Frank Furness. That building, at 220 South 34th Street, is now the Fisher Fine Arts Library. The museum moved here in 1899.

Among the highlights are architectural remains from the ancient Egyptian palace of Merenptah, a 12-ton sphinx, mummies and a crystal ball once owned by China's Dowager Empress. Here, too, is the world's oldest writing, Sumerian cuneiform clay tablets; Nigerian Benin bronzes; and artifacts from Native Alaskan and American Southwest peoples. The museum also has jewels from the royal tombs of the kingdom of Ur, Iraq, dating back 4,500 years, and a single footprint left in clay by a worker at Ur 6,500 years ago. On the second floor are the Penn Museum Shop and the Pepper Mill Café.

❸ Follow 33rd Street north to Penn's **School of Engineering (3)** (*200 South 33rd Street*), home of **ENIAC**, the world's first computer. (By appointment only. Call 215-898-2492.)

Engineers at the school began a secret project during World War II to develop an electronic digital computer. When completed in 1946, it weighed 30 tons, was 80 feet long and contained 18,000 vacuum tubes. Much of ENIAC, which stands for "Electronic Numerical Integrator and Calculator," is at the Smithsonian. But part of it—four of forty panels—is here on display at the school where it was created.

❹ Return to Spruce Street, walk west to 34th Street and turn right to see the **Fisher Fine Arts Library (4)** (*220 South 34th Street, between Walnut and Spruce Streets*). The library is located in a

Fisher Fine
Arts Library

remarkable building designed by famed Philadelphia architect Frank Furness in 1890. (Open 8:30 a.m. to 12 a.m. Monday through Thursday; 8:30 a.m. to 8 p.m. on Friday; 10 a.m. to 8 p.m. Saturday and 10 a.m. to 12 a.m. Sunday. The library serves the teaching, research and scholarly activities of the faculty, students and staff. Access and borrowing privileges are for those carrying a valid Penn Card.)

With its terra-cotta panels, gargoyles and thick columns, this landmark building was somewhat controversial in its time. It also was innovative. The library is said to have been the first to separate the stacks from the reading room. And leaded-glass windows high above provide natural light to study alcoves in the reading room. "Frank Furness, in solving the problems posed by a modern library, also created a work that physically embraces the viewer with great, almost animal-like power—and captures the imagination in the process," wrote David Brownlee of Penn's Art History Department, who calls this his favorite building on campus.

5 Also located in the Furness building is the **Arthur Ross Gallery (5)** (*220 South 34th Street*), the University of Pennsylvania's official art gallery, which displays a variety of paintings, sculpture and ceramics. (Open 10 a.m. to 5 p.m. Tuesday, Thursday and Friday; 10 a.m. to 7 p.m. on Wednesday, and noon to 5 p.m. on weekends. Admission is free.)

Irvine Auditorium

The exhibitions are made up of objects from the university's collection and loans from public and private collections. Tours, lectures, films, children's programs and other events are offered. The gallery usually has four to six major exhibitions a year.

6 Return to Spruce Street and walk west to **Irvine Auditorium (6)** (*Spruce Street between 34th and 36th Streets*), an ornate building designed by the firm of architect Horace Trumbauer and erected in 1928. Trumbauer's chief designer, Julian Abele, was the first African American graduate of Penn's School of Architecture (1902). Trumbauer's firm was responsible for such landmarks as the Philadelphia Museum of Art, the Free Library, the Ardrossan estate in Radnor and dozens of other Main Line mansions. This fortress-like building was inspired by Mont-Saint-Michel, the monastery off the coast of France, and has walls four feet thick at its octagonal base. The auditorium is used for commencements, speeches (political figures from Dwight D. Eisenhower to Vice President Albert Gore have spoken here) and musical performances. It also is used for student concerts and plays.

Inside is a pipe organ made up of 10,973 pipes that was donated to the university by Cyrus H.K. Curtis, publisher of the *Saturday Evening Post*. It is said to be the world's largest university-owned pipe organ.

7–**8** Now head west on Spruce Street to the **Main Quadrangle of the University of Pennsylvania (7)** (*between 34th and 36th Streets and Spruce Street and Hamilton Walk*). Reminiscent of the

Main Quadrangle of the University of Pennsylvania

great European universities, the Quad is surrounded by handsome, Gothic-style dormitory buildings and is the heart of campus residential life for many freshmen. Opened in 1896, it has been home to thousands of Penn students. Each year, about 1,200 first-year students move in. The Quad consists of three houses: Fisher Hassenfeld College House, Riepe College House and Ware College House..

Nearby is a statue of **George Whitefield (8)**, an eloquent Methodist minister and fiery evangelist from Britain who stirred religious fervor among American congregations during the Great Awakening of the mid-18th century.

9 Across from the Quadrangle is the **Wistar Institute (9)** (*Spruce Street and 36th Street Walk*), the oldest independent medical research institute in the United States. (Open 8:30 a.m. to 5 p.m. Monday through Friday. Tours by appointment only. Call 215-898-3700.)

Founded in 1892, the famous institute is named for Caspar Wistar, a prominent Philadelphia physician who wrote the first standard American text on anatomy and was chairman of the Department of Anatomy at Penn's School of Medicine in the early 1800s. In the 1950s, Wistar's scientists developed vaccines for rabies, rubella and other viral diseases, and in the 1970s Wistar was one of the first facilities to be designated as a federally approved cancer research center. The institute may be most famous, though, for a rat. The "WistaRat" was bred here in 1906 by Helen Dean King, and it revolutionized biomedical science as the first standardized laboratory animal. Wistar estimates that today more than half of all laboratory rats are descendants of the original WistaRat.

10 Walk north on 36th Street to the **University of Pennsylvania's Institute of Contemporary Art (10)** (*118 South 36th Street at Sansom Street*). This is Philadelphia's premier contemporary art museum, offering changing exhibits of new artists. (Open 11 a.m. to 8 p.m. Wednesday and 11 a.m. to 6 p.m. Thursday through Sunday. Admission is free.) The museum has shown the work of such artists as Laurie Anderson and Andy Warhol.

11 From contemporary art to contemporary architecture, let's look at one of the most influential buildings of the post–World War II era, by internationally acclaimed architect Louis Kahn. Head south on 36th Street, cross Walnut Street and follow the 36th Street Walk to Hamilton Walk. Make a right turn there and walk west to

University of Pennsylvania Institute of Contemporary Art

the **Richards Medical Research Laboratories (11)** (*3700 Hamilton Walk*), Kahn's finest building in Philadelphia. The 10-floor brick structure was completed in 1962. Along with the adjoining Goddard Laboratories, it was designed as a workplace for teams of biomedical researchers.

Kahn, who joined the Penn faculty in 1957, received international acclaim for the Richards building, with its broken roofline of brick towers, rising between concrete piers. That visual signature is repeated in other buildings on campus. Kahn was among the most prominent architects of his time, yet the Richards building is one of very few local works by the architect, who lived most of his life here.

His influence as a teacher was widespread. Kahn's major buildings include the Mellon Gallery at Yale, the Salk Institute at La Jolla, California, an art museum in Fort Worth and a government complex at Dacca, India. He died while returning home from a trip to India in 1974.

A surprising discovery awaits you at the rear of the Richards building—a picturesque pond and botanical garden that seem like a quiet oasis on the bustling campus.

12 Continue west on Hamilton Walk, turn right on 38th Street, follow it to Locust Walk and turn left there for **St. Mary's**

Church (12) (*3916 Locust Walk near 40th Street*), an Episcopal church that was built in 1872 and serves the surrounding Hamilton Village and University City area. (Sunday Mass with choir 11 a.m. Church office hours 9 a.m. to 2 p.m. Tuesday through Friday and by appointment. Phone 215-386-3916.)

In the 19th century, the church, with its square tower, became the spiritual center of a small group of people who left the city to flee the heat and odors of summer. Much of the land in the area was owned by William Hamilton, a grandnephew of Alexander Hamilton. He divided the acreage into some of the first suburban lots in the country. His development became known as Hamilton Village. The church's altar was built in Rome and was exhibited during the nation's 1876 Centennial celebration in Philadelphia.

13 Walk south on 40th Street, west on Baltimore Avenue and south on Woodland Terrace to **Woodlands Cemetery (13)** (4000 *Woodland Avenue*), a historic necropolis where more than 29,000 people are buried amid a forest of stone monuments along the banks of the Schuylkill. Located in the cemetery is **The Woodlands (13)**, a mansion built between 1786 and 1793 by William Hamilton. The house incorporated a smaller farmhouse erected earlier by his grandfather, Andrew Hamilton, speaker of the Pennsylvania Assembly and designer of Independence Hall. It now serves as the administrative office of the cemetery. (The cemetery is open from dawn to dusk daily. Free. Call ahead for a tour of the mansion: 215-386-2181. Admission $10; seniors and students $8. Visit the website for more information, woodlandsphila.org.)

For many people, the cemetery may seem a forgotten place, reserved for the dead. But for those who look closer, it is a great museum of Philadelphia history, a sculpture garden, a bird sanctuary and a park for strolling. Along the winding lanes are the final resting places of Thomas Eakins, the famed artist; Samuel David Gross, a pioneering surgeon; Anthony Joseph Drexel, founder of Drexel University; and Rembrandt Peale, portrait and historical painter, to name just a few well-known figures buried here.

Woodlands is a focal point of life in this community. Students from the University of Pennsylvania sometimes come here to study on a nice afternoon, local residents take leisurely walks, and history buffs can see Americans' changing attitudes toward death in the tombstones—from the Victorian age, when people erected magnifi-

Woodlands
Cemetery

cent monuments, to modern times, when they install simple markers that are easy to maintain.

Stroll down a brick pathway here, past brooding statues and massive mausoleums resembling Roman and Gothic churches. Nearby, the figure of a child reclines on a marble base, an angel extends his wings and a monument modeled after a church spire rises skyward.

Down one pathway is the grave of Civil War general David Bell Birney, marked by a white marble obelisk. The names of battles and the image of a sword, so carefully carved by a stonecutter long ago, are fading away. But Birney, commander of Pennsylvania volunteers and son of abolitionist James G. Birney, is not forgotten. He fought at Gettysburg, Fredericksburg, Spotsylvania and more than a dozen other battles. And when he died of malaria in 1864, his last words were "Boys! Keep your eyes on that flag!"

Woodlands Cemetery

Some monuments, such as the beautiful marble obelisk marking Commodore David Porter's grave, have been restored. Porter was a naval officer who was probably best known as the commander of the *Essex*, which took nine British ships during the War of 1812. "He was on all occasions among the bravest of the brave," reads one inscription. "Zealous in the performance of every duty, ardent, resolute in trying hours of calamity and steady in the blaze of victory . . . Commodore David Porter. One of the most heroic sons of Pennsylvania."

Porter served aboard the *Constellation* in 1798 and played an important role in its victorious battle with the French frigate *Insurgente*. Later, in the war against Tripoli pirates preying on Mediterranean shipping, he was wounded twice while leading a successful attack and was captured in another operation and imprisoned for 18 months.

Another large monument, topped by an urn, marks the grave of Samuel Gross, author, professor at Jefferson Medical College and founder of the American Medical Association. Gross also is known as the subject of Thomas Eakins' masterpiece painting, *The Gross Clinic*. The urn and obelisk are symbols of death.

Unlike the surgeon's monument, Eakins' grave is marked by a simple block of granite lying flat against the ground. Eakins was perhaps America's finest realist painter, portraitist and sculptor. His ashes and those of his wife, Susan MacDowell Eakins, who was also an accomplished artist, are interred together.

Probably the most elaborate grave belongs to Francis Martin Drexel, father of Anthony Joseph Drexel, the university founder. His huge, classical mausoleum sits in front of the stately Woodlands mansion. Behind ornate bronze doors, a bust of Drexel is bathed in blue light, shining through a stained-glass skylight.

14 On Woodland Avenue, head west to 43rd Street and make a right turn there for the **Marvin Samson Center for the History of Pharmacy (14)** (*600 South 43rd Street*), a museum located in Griffin Hall on the campus of the **University of the Sciences in Philadelphia**. (Open 9 a.m. to 5 p.m. Monday through Thursday; Monday through Friday during the academic year.)

The center was founded in 1821 as the Philadelphia College of Pharmacy. With its restored oak display cases, inlaid floors and decorative metal ceiling, the museum's interior resembles a pharmacy from a century ago. The artifacts here include botanical collections, antique scales, patent medicines, ceramic apothecary jars, and mortars and pestles.

15 Need a break from walking? Get in a car and take a quick drive to **Historic Bartram's Garden (15)** (*54th Street and Lindbergh Boulevard in Southwest Philadelphia*), America's oldest surviving botanical garden. The 45-acre National Historic Landmark includes

Historic Bartram's Garden

John Bartram's 18th-century farmhouse, barn and outbuildings, plus walkways through lovely flower beds. (Grounds are open and free from 10 a.m. to 4 p.m. weekdays and 10 a.m. to 6 p.m. on weekends. House tours noon and 2 p.m. Thursday through Sunday. Admission, $12 adults; $10 seniors and students. Garden tours, 1 and 3 p.m. Thursday through Sunday, $12 adults and $10 seniors and students.)

John Bartram, a botanical genius who served as Royal Botanist for America to King George III, collected many species of plants throughout the American colonies and shared his findings with other botanists around the world. Visitors can now enjoy the fruits of his labors while touring the grounds. You will see Bartram's house, with its mix of classical and colonial styles, the flower gardens, historic trees, a wildflower meadow, river trail and wetlands. The site offers a children's program, workshops, festivals, lectures and an annual plant sale.

It's all worth seeing, and a lovely way to conclude our tour of West Philadelphia.

The Benjamin Franklin Parkway

The Benjamin Franklin Parkway

1 John F. Kennedy Plaza (LOVE Park)

2 Monument to Six Million Jewish Martyrs

3 Thaddeus Kosciuszko statue

4 Copernicus memorial

5 Cathedral Basilica of SS. Peter and Paul

6 Statues of Jesus Breaking Bread, Thomas FitzSimons and Diego de Gardoqui

7 Galusha Pennypacker statue

8 Logan Circle

9 Free Library of Philadelphia

10 Shakespeare Memorial

11 Academy of Natural Sciences of Drexel University

12 Franklin Institute Science Museum

13 All Wars Memorial to Colored Soldiers and Sailors and Civil War memorials

14 Francisco de Miranda statue

15 Barnes Foundation

16 Rodin Museum

17 Eastern State Penitentiary

18 Eakins Oval

19 Philadelphia Museum of Art

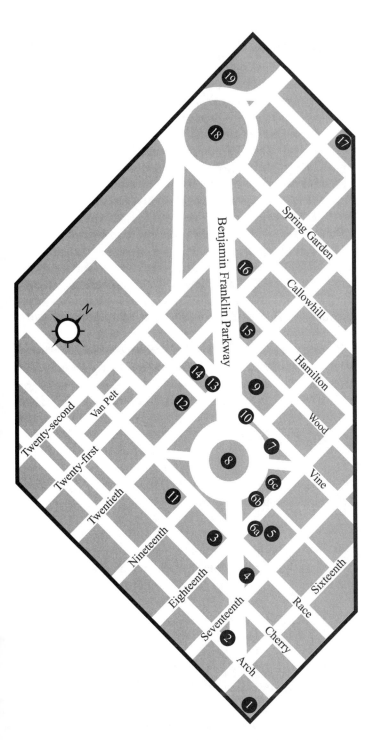

Benjamin Franklin Parkway

Spring Garden

Callowhill

Hamilton

Wood

Vine

Race

Cherry

Arch

Seventeenth

Eighteenth

Nineteenth

Twentieth

Twenty-first

Twenty-second

Van Pelt

Sixteenth

N

USEFUL INFORMATION

Restaurants handy to the Parkway include Franklin Food-works, a large, sunny cafeteria in the Franklin Institute, 20th Street and the Benjamin Franklin Parkway; Stir, the only Frank Gehry–designed restaurant in the Northeast, located in the main building of the Philadelphia Museum of Art, 2600 Benjamin Franklin Parkway; Rose Tattoo, 1847 Callowhill Street; the Garden Restaurant at the Barnes Foundation, 2025 Benjamin Franklin Parkway; and City Tap House–Logan Square, 100 North 18th Street.

For getting around, the PHLASH shuttle bus can be useful. The bus makes stops at the John F. Kennedy Plaza at 16th Street and John F. Kennedy Boulevard; 17th Street and Kennedy Boulevard; 17th and the Parkway; 18th Street and the Parkway; 21st Street and the Parkway; and the Philadelphia Museum of Art. SEPTA buses 7, 32, 38, 43, 48 and 76 also serve the area.

Parking is available at meters and at several area facilities, including 19th Street near Cherry Street and 21st Street near Race Street.

Introduction

The Benjamin Franklin Parkway is often called the Champs-Élysées of Philadelphia. And rightfully so. The 250-foot-wide parkway— with its fountains, statues and cultural institutions—was inspired by the grand boulevard of Paris and is one of the most attractive places in the city.

The tree-lined boulevard juts out of Fairmount Park and cuts deep into the heart of the city. At its western end, atop a high elevation, sits the temple-like Philadelphia Museum of Art. At its eastern end rises the tower of City Hall. And in between, along the Parkway's 1.2-mile length, are more museums, the colorful flags of many nations, and small parks festooned with flowers, fountains and monuments. The surroundings have made the Parkway a popular location for parades, festivals, fireworks and on-location shots for movies.

The idea of a parkway was first proposed about 1902 and pushed by civic leader Eli Kirk Price II, who worked to clear the way with municipal authorities. French architects Jacques-Henri-Auguste Gréber and Paul Cret designed the grand boulevard, and work finally began in 1917. It was a departure from the original grid system laid out for William Penn's Philadelphia, and what a dramatic change! Gréber and Cret also designed one of the Parkway's great cultural institutions, the Rodin Museum. Other Cret works include the plaza, pool and entrances to Rittenhouse Square, the Benjamin Franklin Bridge and the Federal Reserve Bank at 10th and Chestnut Streets.

The Parkway and its cultural adornments were years in the making. The Free Library of Philadelphia, on the north side of the Parkway at 19th Street, opened in 1927. It was designed by Horace Trumbauer as a replica of the Château Crillon on the Place de la Concorde in Paris. The imposing Philadelphia Museum of Art opened in 1928. The neoclassical building also was designed by Trumbauer's firm and was erected on the site of the old reservoir. The cornerstone of the Franklin Institute, at 20th Street and the Parkway, was laid in 1932, adding yet another cultural institution. Apartment houses

The Benjamin
Franklin
Parkway

went up over the years, although they generally have been screened by the growth of trees.

The Parkway is one of the city's grand processional routes and has hosted the Columbus, Thanksgiving, St. Patrick's Day, Pulaski Day and Veterans Day parades. It has also been the site of visits by the Pope and of other large public events including Super Sunday in October, when hundreds of thousands of people turned out for food, concerts and other entertainment.

But urban planners see much more in the parkway's future. They submitted plans to make the Parkway more accessible and useable for pedestrians and for entertaining. One of the three plazas along the boulevard, John F. Kennedy Plaza, better known as LOVE Park at 16th Street and John F. Kennedy Boulevard, received $26 million in renovations and reopened in 2018 with a water fountain, new green space and underground parking garage. Logan Circle, meanwhile, is set to return to being a square, as William Penn envisioned, and exhibits and pavilions are to be added. And Eakins Oval has been more family-friendly with lane closures on the Parkway providing extra space for pedestrians, art displays, a seating platform and misting pavilion for cooling off. Both sides of the Parkway are being redeveloped with new or expanded museums and apartments.

The Tour

1 Let's start at the **John F. Kennedy Plaza**, also known as **LOVE Park (1)** (*16th Street and John F. Kennedy Boulevard*), a sprawling park adjacent to City Hall with grassy areas, trees, flowers and a fountain.

Its **LOVE sculpture** by Robert Indiana was purchased and given to the city in 1978 by F. Eugene Dixon. The iconic artwork was recently restored and repainted and adds a splash of color to the surroundings. It's a magnet for visitors who pose with it for photos.

In the southwest corner of the park is an unusual saucer-shaped building: a former welcome center, which is expected to be renovated by 2020 to house a restaurant and seating inside and outside for scores of patrons.

2 Cross 16th Street and begin making your way up the Parkway. On the south side is the **Monument to Six Million Jew-**

Monument
to Six Million
Jewish Martyrs

ish Martyrs (2) killed by the Nazis from 1933 to 1945 (*Arch and 16th Streets at the Parkway*).

The Holocaust monument, created in 1964 by Nathan Rapoport, depicts figures struggling for freedom. "Now and forever enshrined in memory are the six million Jewish martyrs who perished in concentration camps, ghettos and gas chambers," says the inscription. "In their deepest agony they clung to the image of humanity, and their acts of resistance in the forests and ghettos redeemed the honor of man," reads a portion of the text.

❸ Farther along the south side of the Parkway is a heroic statue honoring **Thaddeus Kosciuszko (3)** (*18th Street and the Parkway*), the Polish military hero who helped the former colonies fight for their freedom from Britain.

The statue by Marian Konieczny was given to the United States by the Polish people in 1976 to mark the nation's 200 years of independence. It shows Gen. Kosciuszko in uniform with a sword at his side. (The inscription renders his name as Tadeusz Kosciuszko.)

4 Nearby, on the north side of the Parkway, is a metal and stone memorial honoring **Copernicus (4)** *(near 18th Street and the Parkway)*, the great Polish astronomer. Copernicus (the Polish spelling Kopernik is used here) was born in Torun in 1473, and soil from his birthplace was placed here. The monument was a gift to the city from the Polish-American community in 1973.

5 Continue to walk along the north side of the Parkway to the front of the **Cathedral Basilica of SS. Peter and Paul (5)** *(18th Street at the Parkway)*, the spiritual center for more than one million Roman Catholics in the Philadelphia area. (Open daily. Masses scheduled at 7:15 a.m. and 12:05 p.m. Monday through Friday in the Cathedral Chapel; 12:05 Saturday in the Cathedral Chapel and 5:15

Cathedral Basilica of SS. Peter and Paul

p.m. Saturday in the Basilica; and 8, 9:30 and 11 a.m. and 6:30 p.m. Sunday in the Basilica. Spanish Mass in the Cathedral Chapel at 12:30 p.m. Sunday.) The Italian Renaissance–style cathedral was designed by architects Napoleon Le Brun and John Notman and was erected between 1846 and 1864. The fortress-like structure was conceived in the wake of the city's anti-Catholic riots of 1844. With its copper dome and imposing sandstone exterior, the cathedral dominates Logan Circle. Its interior is spacious, with half-ton bronze chandeliers lighting the sanctuary and a vaulted ceiling rising 80 feet. A red marble canopy was placed over the main altar in 1887.

Shortly after it was completed, the cathedral overlooked the Great Central Fair, held from June 7 to 21, 1864. The event was sponsored by the U.S. Sanitary Commission and raised more than $1 million for the care of soldiers and sailors wounded in the Civil War. Thousands of people enjoyed amusements and admired a collection of paintings and exhibits, including a horseshoe machine, wax fruit and glass-blowing demonstrations. The crowd also saw the recently renominated President Lincoln and the First Lady, who visited the fair on June 16.

6 Located around the cathedral are several interesting sculptures. A solitary statue of **Jesus Breaking Bread (6)** (*Parkway and 18th Street*) stands next to the church, facing the Parkway. And in a small park across from the front entrance to SS. Peter and Paul is a statue of **Thomas FitzSimons (6)** (*18th Street between the Parkway and Vine Street*), a member of the Continental Congress and signer of the Constitution, who is buried in St. Mary's burying ground. Fitz-Simons was born in Ireland in 1741 and died in Philadelphia in 1811.

Looking north from the FitzSimons statue you'll see another grassy area, site of a statue of **Diego de Gardoqui (6)** (*near 18th and Vine Streets*), envoy of the King of Spain during the 18th century. He was born in 1735 and died in 1798. The statue was presented to the city by King Juan Carlos of Spain in 1976 during the nation's Bicentennial.

7 A few steps farther on—moving around the outer edge of Logan Circle—is a statue honoring **Galusha Pennypacker (7)** (*near Vine Street and the Parkway in front of the former Family Court building*), a Union general who distinguished himself for heroism during the Civil War. In 1862, at age 20, Pennypacker was the youngest federal general of the era. He was wounded four times during fighting around Petersburg, Virginia, in 1864 and wounded again during the capture of the Confederate Fort Fisher near Wilmington, North Carolina, in 1865. But he lived out the war and then some, dying in 1916. The statue depicts a warrior flanked by two lions.

8 Now cross the Parkway to **Logan Circle (8)** (*18th Street and the Parkway*), one of William Penn's five original squares and the site of the **Swann Memorial Fountain** by Alexander Stirling Calder.

The square served as a burying ground, a pasture in the early 1820s and a site of public executions. William Gross was the last person hanged here, in 1823. The square was named for Penn's secretary, James Logan, in 1825.

Today, the Swann fountain, opened in 1924, is the focus of the circle. The figures depicted represent Philadelphia's three main waterways—the Delaware and Schuylkill Rivers and Wissahickon Creek.

Swann Memorial Fountain

The figures were restored in recent years at a cost of about $2 million. In summer, the fountain is a favorite place for children to cool off. Office workers often fill the area during the lunch break.

9 Head north, crossing Vine Street, then make a left turn for the **Free Library of Philadelphia (9)** (*19th and Vine Streets*), a Greek Revival building housing more than six million books, magazines, newspapers, videos and other materials. (Open 9 a.m. to 9 p.m. Monday through Thursday, 9 a.m. to 6 p.m. Friday, 9 a.m. to 5 p.m. Saturday, and 1 to 5 p.m. Sunday.)

The Rare Book Room has holdings dating back thousands of years, including cuneiform clay tablets, illuminated manuscripts from the Middle Ages, first editions of Charles Dickens and other manuscripts, among them Edgar Allan Poe's *Murders in the Rue Morgue* and "The Raven." The Newspaper Room has major U.S. and foreign papers, including some dating to the colonial era. The library also has much to offer music lovers, including the Edwin S. Fleisher Collection of more than 12,000 musical scores.

10 Before leaving this side of the Parkway, stop briefly outside the library to view the **Shakespeare Memorial (10)** (*near 19th Street, between the Parkway and Vine Street*), called *Hamlet and the Fool*. It was designed by Alexander Stirling Calder, son of Alexander Milne Calder, who created the William Penn statue atop City Hall. The Shakespeare Memorial honors Philadelphia's Shakespearean actors and scholars, the most famous of whom were Edwin Forrest, John Drew, Louisa Lane Drew and Joseph Jefferson.

11 Cross the Parkway to the south side to the **Academy of Natural Sciences of Drexel University (11)** (*1900 Benjamin Franklin Parkway*), the oldest science research institute in the Western Hemisphere and site of popular dinosaur exhibits. (Open 10 a.m. to 4:30 p.m. Monday through Friday and 10 a.m. to 5 p.m. weekends and holidays. Weekday admission $22, age 13 and above; $18 for ages 2 to 12; children under age 2 free; seniors, military service members and students, $19. Save $2 when purchasing tickets online.)

The Academy of Natural Sciences was founded in 1812 and located in a narrow building at Broad and Sansom Streets. It moved to its present location in 1876, and formed an affiliation with Drexel University in 2011. Outside the building is a statue of Joseph Leidy, a renowned 19th-century paleontologist who was president of the

Academy of Natural Sciences of Drexel University

academy and director of the Philadelphia Zoo. Adjacent to his statue is another depicting dinosaurs.

Inside, there are dioramas of stuffed animals and birds from around the world and exhibits of extinct species. See live butterflies in a rain forest setting. You can handle snakes, lizards and tarantulas at the "Outside In" mini-museum. Feast your eyes on the gem and mineral exhibits, but make sure to save time for the dinosaurs— *Tyrannosaurus Rex* and *Gigantosaurus*. You also can visit a working paleontology lab and dig site.

12 A block to the west is the **Franklin Institute Science Museum (12)** (*20th Street and the Parkway*), a marvelous place with many hands-on exhibits and home of the Fels Planetarium. Also here is the Tuttleman IMAX Theater, where movies seem to pull the audience into the action. (Museum open 9:30 a.m. to 5 p.m. daily. Admission ranges from $20 to $35 for adults and $15 to $31 for children, depending on time of day and day of the week.)

The institute was founded in 1824 to honor Benjamin Franklin, whose colossal, 30-foot statue greets visitors. The cornerstone of the present building was set in place in 1932. The Fels Planetarium opened in 1933, and the Science Museum in 1934.

Here, through many clever interactive exhibits, you can experience sounds, energy, motion, electricity and time. Perhaps the most popular exhibit is the world's largest artificial heart, which you can

Franklin Institute Science Museum

walk through, following the route of a corpuscle. See the cockpit of a jet aircraft. Study the stars, explore space and catch a laser show at the Fels Planetarium. Then, take in a movie at the Tuttleman IMAX Theater in the Mandell Center. The 79-foot, domed screen and 56-speaker sound system transport the audience into extreme weather, to the mountains, into outer space and on a spectacular roller-coaster ride.

⓭ Before resuming our Parkway trek, pause at two nearby veterans memorials, one honoring the soldiers and sailors who fought for the Union during the Civil War, and the other commemorating the contribution of African Americans who fought in all U.S. wars. **All Wars Memorial to Colored Soldiers and Sailors (13)** (*20th Street and the Parkway*) sits in a grassy park across from the entrance to the Franklin Institute. Figures represented here depict servicemen in World War I uniforms. But the 1934 memorial honors blacks who served in the Indian Wars, the American Revolution, the Civil War, the Spanish American War, the Philippine Insurrection and World War I. (Many black troops were trained at Camp William Penn in nearby Cheltenham Township, Montgomery County, during the Civil War.)

Nearby, sitting on both sides of the Parkway like bookends, are **Civil War memorials (13)** (*20th Street and the Parkway*). On the north side, the monument depicts a battle scene, with soldiers surrounding a mortar. Below is written: "Each for himself gathered up the cherished purposes of life, its aims and ambitions, its dearest affections, and flung all, with life itself, into the scale of battle."

On the south side of the Parkway, a monument shows sailors, one wounded, alongside an artillery piece. Above are these words: "In giving freedom to the slave, we assure freedom to the free." And below: "All who have labored today in behalf of the Union have wrought for the best interests of the country and the world not only for present but for all future ages."

14 Also on the south side of the Parkway, between the Civil War memorials and the Franklin Institute, is a statue honoring **Francisco de Miranda (14)** (*20th Street and the Parkway*), a native of Caracas, Venezuela, who fought for freedom in the American Revolution, the French Revolution and in Latin America. "There is in the world only one . . . nation in which you can discuss politics outside of the tried heart of a friend," he once said. "That country is the United States." John Adams praised the Venezuelan for his knowledge of war and politics. The statue, depicting Francisco de Miranda stepping forward with his hand on his sword, was presented to the United States in 1976 for the nation's 200th birthday.

15 On the north side of the Parkway between 20th and 21st Streets is the **Barnes Foundation (15)** (*2025 Benjamin Franklin Parkway*), a world-class art museum that moved to its new building in 2012. (Open 11 a.m. to 5 p.m. Wednesday through Monday. Admission is $25 for adults, $23 for seniors, $5 for college students with ID and youths ages 13 to 18.)

The Barnes displays the largest collection of Renoir paintings in the world along with impressionist, post-impressionist and early modernist masterpieces. See the works of Van Gogh, Matisse and Picasso as well as ironwork, African sculpture, Native American ceramics and jewelry and Pennsylvania German furniture.

16 Nearby, on the same side of the Parkway, is the **Rodin Museum (16)** (*22nd Street and the Parkway*), a small but magnificent, gem-like museum featuring the largest collection of Auguste Rodin's sculptures and drawings outside of Paris. The Beaux-Arts-style building and formal French garden provide a refined, elegant environ-

Rodin Museum

ment for 150 of Rodin's marbles, bronzes and plaster. (Open 10 a.m. to 5 p.m. Wednesday through Monday. Admission $12; seniors, $11; students , $7; children 18 and under, free.)

The museum was designed by French architect Paul Cret and opened in 1929. At the entrance, you will ascend the stairs next to the famous statue of *The Thinker*. Pass through the temple-like facade into a formal garden with a lily pool, then head to the portico with the original casting of *The Gates of Hell*, a 21-foot-high sculpture with scores of human and animal figures. The museum contains castings of some of the French master's greatest works: *The Kiss, St. John the Baptist Preaching, The Burghers of Calais* and *Eternal Springtime*.

17 About five blocks north of the Parkway is the **Eastern State Penitentiary (17)** (*22nd Street and Fairmount Avenue*), once the most expensive prison in the nation and one of the most famous penal facilities in the world. (Open 10 a.m. to 5 p.m. daily. Tours on the hour; last tour at 4 p.m. Admission when purchasing tickets on-line $14 for adults; $12 for seniors; $10 for students and children 7 to 12. Not recommended for children under 7. Tickets purchased at the site cost $2 more. Military members with ID receive a $2 discount.)

Eastern State Penitentiary, designed by architect John Haviland, was built between 1823 and 1829 and became the model for more than 300 prisons all over the world. Seven rows of cells radiate out from a central administration building/tower like spokes of a wagon wheel. The massive outer wall is 12 feet thick at its base and runs 30 feet high, with towers at the corners and a fortress-like entrance.

The prisoners here were kept alone in a cell with nothing but a bed, a Bible and a skylight. The confinement was ordered to prevent inmates from being bad influences on one another and to give them time to consider their offenses. In a visit to America in 1842, the great English novelist Charles Dickens most wanted to see two things: Niagara Falls and Eastern State. Dickens, though, criticized the isolation as cruel. "I hold this slow and daily tampering with the mysteries of the brain to be immeasurably worse than any torture of the body," he wrote. In the same era, Alexis de Tocqueville, who was chronicling life in the United States, praised the prison for its reliance on psychological, rather than physical, punishment. The system of solitary confinement was officially abandoned in 1913.

Over the years, the prison held some of the nation's most notorious criminals. Al Capone sat out a gang war here, partying with prison guards in a cell furnished with antique furniture, oil paintings and oriental rugs. Capone served eight months in 1929 and 1930 on a gun charge. The prison also held bank robber Willie Sutton, who joined 11 other men in tunneling under the wall in 1945. They were quickly recaptured.

The most popular stops on tours of this eerie, crumbling prison are Capone's cell, which is decorated in 1920s opulence, and Death Row, which opened for public tours for the first time in 1999.

18 Head back to the Parkway and **Eakins Oval (18)** (*in front of the Philadelphia Museum of Art at Spring Garden Street*), a plaza named for Philadelphia's most famous painter, Thomas Eakins.

The plaza has three fountains. One displays an equestrian statue of George Washington. Four figures and animals look over pools representing four important American waterways: the Mississippi, the Potomac, the Hudson and the Delaware. Another fountain honors Eli Kirk Price, who worked hard to make the Parkway a reality. A third honors John Ericsson, an inventor and naval architect who developed the ironclad ship *Monitor*, which fought a famous Civil War battle against another ironclad vessel, the *Merrimac*, at Hampton Roads, Virginia, in 1862.

Philadelphia Museum of Art

19 Cross over to the **Philadelphia Museum of Art (19)** (*2600 Benjamin Franklin Parkway*), a neoclassical building that contains spectacular art collections from Europe, Asia and the United States covering more than 2,000 years. (Open 10 a.m. to 5 p.m. Tuesday through Sunday, until 8:45 p.m. on Wednesdays and Fridays. Closed Mondays and major holidays. Admission $25 for adults; $23 for seniors over 65; $14 for students with ID. Pay what you wish 10 a.m. to 5 p.m. on the first Sunday of the month and from 5 to 8:45 p.m. every Wednesday.)

The museum was modeled after an ancient Greek temple and constructed of Minnesota dolomite. It was begun in 1919, and the first section opened in 1928. Ascend the 72 steps (made famous by the movie hero Rocky, whose statue is at the bottom of the steps),

Statue of Rocky in front of the Philadelphia Museum of Art

Great Stair
Hall inside the
Philadelphia
Museum of Art

taking in the splendid details of the building—the great columns
and pediments. At the top of the steps, turn and look back down the
Parkway at the city skyline.

Inside, walk through the glorious Great Stair Hall, graced by
Saint-Gaudens' statue of *Diana*, then head into the galleries—200 of
them. Among the major collections are Western art from the Renaissance to the 1800s; modern and contemporary works by such artists
as Picasso and Matisse; Impressionist and Post-Impressionist work,
interspersed with sculptures by Degas, Rodin and Brancusi.

Some of the "don't-miss" works here are Marcel Duchamp's *Nude
Descending a Staircase* (which scandalized the 1913 Armory Show in
New York), Thomas Eakins' *The Concert Singer*, Pablo Picasso's *Three
Musicians*, Benjamin West's *Benjamin Franklin Drawing Electricity from
the Sky*, Paul Cézanne's *The Large Bathers* and Vincent Van Gogh's
Sunflowers.

Many of the collections of paintings, prints, sculpture, furniture
and glasswork are in special settings. A French medieval cloister
and a 14th-century chapel are among the most handsome. There are
striking tapestries, stained glass, stone carvings and armor displays.

The museum's 18th-century English and French period rooms display gilt items and elegant furniture. Other rooms take you through a Chinese palace hall, a stone temple from India and a Japanese teahouse in a bamboo garden. The Museum of Art also has a second building. Take a brief walk north of the museum, cross Kelly Drive and follow Pennsylvania Avenue to the Perelman Building (*2525 Pennsylvania Avenue at Fairmount Avenue*), an annex of the museum that displays cutting-edge photography, textiles, fashion, and contemporary art and design in three main galleries. (The Art Deco building is open 10 a.m. to 5 p.m. Tuesday through Sunday. Access is included in the general admission to the Museum of Art.)

A full day is hardly enough time to taste the joys of these wonderful attractions, so plan on a return visit. Also make sure to take in the vista of the Schuylkill and Boathouse Row from the west-facing back entrance to the Art Museum. The gardens of Fairmount Park spread out below the museum, with benches and shade trees. Sit and relax here, after your day of touring the treasures of the Benjamin Franklin Parkway.

Philadelphia's Backyard: Fairmount Park

Philadelphia's Backyard: Fairmount Park

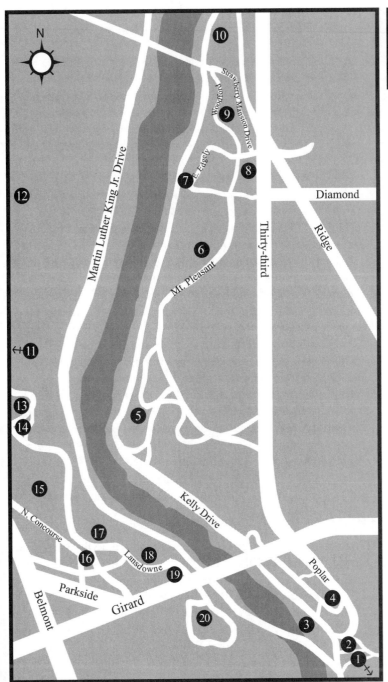

USEFUL INFORMATION

A s you explore the park, consider taking a picnic basket—there are many beautiful settings for lunch. Choose a spot along the Schuylkill. Watch the rowing teams. Take in some art. There are more than 200 statues by noted sculptors.

If you stop in at the Philadelphia Museum of Art, you'll find lovely, full-service dining at the Cafe and the Stir restaurant. The Philadelphia Zoo also has restaurants.

The park is wonderful for walking, jogging, biking, skating—and driving. But for those looking for public transportation and a narrated tour, try the Philadelphia Trolley Works (215-389-8687). Victorian trolley-style buses leave from the John F. Kennedy Plaza at 16th Street and John F. Kennedy Boulevard; the Perelman Building of the Philadelphia Museum of Art at Fairmount and Pennsylvania Avenues; the east entrance of the Philadelphia Museum of Art at Eakins Oval; Memorial Hall/Please Touch Museum at East Memorial Hall Drive and Avenue of the Republic; and the Philadelphia Zoo, 34th Street and Girard Avenue, among other stops. SEPTA's distinctive-looking, purple PHLASH buses travel from Center City to the rear of the museum, and the transit agency's buses also run through the park. For instance, bus route 32 runs from Center City to Lemon Hill, Woodford Mansion and Strawberry Mansion. It can be boarded on Broad Street, between Spruce and City Hall, and also on John F. Kennedy Boulevard between 15th and 16th Streets.

Introduction

The name first appeared on plans for the city more than three hundred years ago. William Penn's surveyor, Thomas Holme, spotted a piece of high ground—where the Philadelphia Museum of Art now stands—and he called it "Faire Mount."

The name stuck. City officials began using it in the mid-1800s for the park, which by 1855 encompassed 2,000 acres and had become a model for city parks around the world. Penn's effort to create a "Greene Country Towne" had begun in 1682 with the laying out of five squares. Four of them—Washington, Franklin, Rittenhouse and

Logan Squares—remain part of Fairmount Park. The fifth, Centre Square, is the site of City Hall.

Beyond the squares, five acres were set aside by city officials along the east bank of the Schuylkill in 1812 for the Fairmount Water Works. A dam was constructed, along with a pumping station, which diverted water to a reservoir on higher ground, where the art museum stands today. Water was piped from there into the city. The genius was in concealing the pump house in a set of buildings that look like Greek temples.

"It would be considered the absence of all taste for a stranger to appear in Philadelphia and not devote an hour to visit the Fairmount Waterworks," said the publication *Views of Philadelphia* in 1838. The picturesque site was visited by thousands of Americans and people from overseas, including Charles Dickens, who toured it in 1842.

Over the years, more ground was added to the park, on both sides of the Schuylkill. Other people had been purchasing land along the river, too. Industries soon were discharging waste into the water that was heading to the reservoir. The city and state had to take action to save Penn's dream of a verdant town. A bill was introduced in the state legislature in 1865 to authorize the purchase of ground along the west bank of the river.

"You have it in your power, by saying *aye* upon this bill, to give Philadelphia as fair a landscape and as charming a scene as ever gladdened the eye of mortal man since the gates of Eden were closed to human eyes," said Pennsylvania Assemblyman John Miller in his eloquent defense of the measure.

The legislature established the Fairmount Park Commission two years later and authorized the purchase of land "to be laid out and maintained forever as an open public place and park, for the health and enjoyment of the people . . . and the preservation of the water supply." It worked for another 40 years or so, but by 1909 the Schuylkill was so polluted that the water works was shut down.

The growing park became the site in 1876 of the mammoth national Centennial Exhibition, which celebrated the 100th anniversary of the founding of the nation. More than 200 buildings were erected on about 250 acres in West Fairmount Park. Two notable buildings from the event remain: Memorial Hall, with its beautiful green dome, and the Ohio House.

Years after the Centennial Exhibition, the much-traveled writer Lafcadio Hearn wrote: "Is it possible you have never seen Fairmount Park? Believe me, then, that it is the most beautiful place of the whole civilized world. . . . Your Central Park [in New York City] is a cabbage garden by comparison."

The park contains about 70 historically certified buildings, including the largest collection of late-18th- to early-19th-century villas and country houses in the United States. The houses have cantilevered balconies, decorative gables, walk-in fireplaces, carved moldings and paneled walls. They represent more than two centuries of Philadelphia history in wood, stone and Wissahickon schist. Call ahead to these sites or to the Philadelphia Department of Parks and Recreation (215-683-3600) before visiting. Admission costs and days and hours of operation vary.

The park also takes in the oldest zoo in the nation, first opened in 1874; Boathouse Row, the clubhouses of rowing organizations, flanking the nation's finest rowing course; the Mann Center for the Performing Arts, summer home of the Philadelphia Orchestra; and the Dell Music Center, an outdoor entertainment venue, site of music and ethnic programs.

For many visitors, though, the strongest lures are nature and the myriad of recreation facilities. Here is America's largest landscaped park—8,900 acres, about 10 percent of the city. Within this sprawling acreage are 73 baseball and softball diamonds, 105 tennis courts, 13 football fields, 14 soccer fields, two cricket fields, two field-hockey fields, a rugby field, a bowling green, three bocce courts, six golf courses, six indoor recreation centers, three outdoor swimming pools and one indoor pool, 100 miles of bridle paths and hiking trails, 25 miles of paved bikeways and a fishing stream stocked with trout each season.

In the northwestern section of the park is a lush, green valley created by the Wissahickon Creek as it moves south toward the Schuylkill. "Wissahickon" is a combination of two words used by the Lenape Indians for the creek: "Wisauksickan," which means yellow-colored stream, and "Wisamickan," or catfish creek. It runs 21 miles, the last seven miles inside the city limits. Several inns were located along the creek over the past two centuries. Two of the buildings remain. One is now used as a police station; the other is the Valley Green Inn, Springfield Avenue and Wissahickon Creek, which was built in 1850. The Wissahickon Valley is a perfect spot to relax amid natural beauty. Forbidden Drive, a dirt-and-gravel path, runs along the west side of the creek and is used by joggers, hikers, horseback riders and fishermen.

Because of the park's vast size, it is impossible to do this tour all by foot. So take your car, and park near the back of the art museum. Then you have two choices: You can do the walking and driving tour, or you can pick up one of the motorized park trolleys for a narrated tour. The trolleys leave from the west entrance of the art museum.

The Tour

1-2 Let's begin at the **John F. Kennedy Plaza (1)** (*16th Street and John F. Kennedy Boulevard*), where you can pick up a motorized trolley. You can also board the trolley at the east entrance to the **Philadelphia Museum of Art (2)** (*2600 Benjamin Franklin Parkway*) and at the nearby **Perelman Building**, an annex of the Philadelphia Museum of Art at 2525 Pennsylvania Avenue. If you're driving, park behind the art museum. While you're there, stroll through the lovely **Azalea Garden** and relax on one of the benches while enjoying the colorful view.

Then head for one of the city's great landmarks, the **Fairmount Water Works** (*between the Museum of Art and Boathouse Row, East Fairmount Park*), a grouping of Greek Revival buildings marking the water-pumping station that supplied water to the city throughout most of the 19th century. A National Historic, Civil and Mechanical Landmark, it is also on the National Register of Historic Places. (Open 10 a.m. to 5 p.m. Tuesday through Saturday and 1 to 5 p.m. on Sunday. General admission free. Donations are recommended for tour groups outside of Philadelphia: $10 for adults; $6 for students, $10 after business hours. Two hours of free parking available along Waterworks Drive.)

The water works was designed in 1812 by Frederick Graff, who served as chief of the great works project for many years. The temples and mill house facades were built between 1819 and 1822 in a mix of styles—Federal and Gothic, Roman and Greek Revival. They covered steam engines, water wheels and water turbines. Water was pumped from these works to a reservoir on top of Faire Mount, then it flowed downhill from there through wooden pipes to Centre Square (where City Hall stands today) for distribution.

The city later moved a fountain, with the *Allegory of the Schuylkill River* sculpture by William Rush, from the works' engine house at Centre Square to Fairmount and laid out gardens and walkways that were the beginning of one of the largest landscaped parks in the world. Over time, Rush's original *Allegory* sculpture deteriorated, but a bronze cast now stands near the water works, where it is popularly known as *Water Nymph and Bittern.*

Across the river, the view of the water works and the nearby waterfall is splendid, a must-see for any visitor.

From the water works, walk past the nearby **Italian Fountain**, also called *The Fountain of the Sea Horses,* a gift from Italy to mark the Sesquicentennial. Then, before heading west on Kelly Drive, pause to admire the handsome bronze statue of **Lincoln the Emancipator** by Randolph Rogers.

3 To the west of the Fairmount Water Works is **Boathouse Row (3)** (*Kelly Drive, East Fairmount Park*), a cluster of 19th-century houses of various styles that are home to the rowing clubs of the "Schuylkill Navy." The row begins with Lloyd Hall, the only one of the buildings that is open to the public.

The rowing clubs are part of a private boating organization that traces its roots back to 1858. Their 11 Gothic Revival, Victorian Gothic and Italianate-style houses are outlined with small lights that make for a spectacular view from across the river at night.

Walking further along Kelly Drive will bring you to the **Ellen Phillips Samuel Memorial Sculpture Garden**, where you can see the works of more than a dozen artists. This is a beautiful walk out past the boathouses and leads to the most popular running trail in the city, along the east bank of the Schuylkill. Runners, in-line skaters, bikers and mothers pushing baby strollers share the pathways.

4 Once you've absorbed the ambience of Boathouse Row, head back for your car. We're about to tour some of Philadelphia's grandest houses of the 18th and 19th centuries, up on the bluffs overlooking the Schuylkill. The mansions of Fairmount Park—some owned by the city, others owned or managed by civic groups—constitute the largest collection of houses from this period in the country. Many are open for tours, but it's best to contact the site or Philadelphia Department of Parks and Recreation (215-683-3600) beforehand. Visitors can buy tickets at the houses for single, or multiple-house, tours.

Drive west on Kelly Drive to the end of Boathouse Row, where you will make a right turn and follow a road around to the right to

Lemon Hill (4) (*Sedgley and Lemon Hill Drives, off Poplar Drive, East Fairmount Park*). This is an Adamesque Federal-style country house completed in 1800 by Henry Pratt, a successful merchant and owner of many properties in Philadelphia. (Open 10 a.m. to 4 p.m. Thursday through Sunday, April through December, and by appointment only January through March. Admission is $8 for adults; $5 for seniors over 65, students with ID and youths 13 to 17; and free for children 12 and under. For more information, call 215-232-4337.)

Robert Morris, one of the signers of the Declaration of Independence and a financier of the Revolution, built a farm and elaborate greenhouse at the site in 1770. He called it "The Hills." But by the end of the century, Morris, a close friend of George Washington, had overextended himself and his land was confiscated.

Henry Pratt, son of portrait painter Matthew Pratt, purchased nearly 43 acres of Morris' 300-acre property. Lemon trees were growing in the large greenhouse, and the estate became known as "Lemon Hill." Pratt built the present house between 1799 and 1800 but probably did not live here. It has a pair of curving steps leading to double doors on the north side. The entry hall has a checkerboard floor of Valley Forge marble. The south facade enclosed oval salons on three floors, with unusual curved walls, doors and windows.

5 Return to Kelly Drive, make a right turn and follow the road past the **Glendinning Rock Garden** and Frederic Remington's equestrian statue **Cowboy**, set high on a rock outcropping. Driving further, you'll come upon a second equestrian statue—this one of **Ulysses S. Grant**—at Fountain Green Drive. Turn right here, then left at the next street, which will take you to **Mount Pleasant (5)** (*Mount Pleasant Drive, East Fairmount Park*), a charming Georgian mansion that had several famous owners, including Benedict Arnold, the Revolutionary War–era traitor. (At the time of this writing, Mount Pleasant was undergoing general maintenance. Check with the Philadelphia Museum of Art for scheduling and ticket costs: 215-763-8100.)

Once described by John Adams as "the most elegant seat in Pennsylvania," Mount Pleasant was built between 1761 and 1762 by sea captain John Macpherson, a Scot who made his fortune as a privateer. It has ornate woodwork, Chippendale-style furnishings and eight fireplaces. One of the more interesting characteristics of the house is its symmetry. False doors in a first-floor parlor mimic the doors leading to the room, and arched windows face each other on both sides of the house.

The house later was owned by Benedict Arnold, who bought it as a wedding present for his bride, Peggy Shippen, but was found guilty of treason and fled the country before he could occupy the property. Jonathan Williams, first superintendent of West Point and a great-nephew of Benjamin Franklin, also owned it.

❻ As you follow Mount Pleasant Drive, you will pass **Rockland Mansion**, a Federal-style house built by George Thompson in 1810 and restored to serve as the home of the Psychoanalytic Center of Philadelphia. Make a left turn at the next street, Reservoir Drive, and then look to your left. Here is **Ormiston (6)** (*2000 Reservoir Drive near Mount Pleasant Drive, East Fairmount Park*), a red brick Georgian house built in 1798 by lawyer Edward Burd. (For more information, check with the Royal Heritage Society at info@ormistonrhs.org or the Philadelphia Department of Parks and Recreation at 215-683-3600.)

Burd named the house for his grandfather's country seat near Edinburgh, Scotland. It is furnished in reproduction 18th- and 19th-century furniture. The Royal Heritage Society of Delaware Valley occupies the house and provides tours. Exhibits and events here focus on British heritage in the region.

❼ Make a left turn from the parking lot next to Ormiston, follow Reservoir Drive to the next cross street, Randolph Drive, and make another left for **Laurel Hill (7)** (*7201 Randolph Drive near Reservoir Drive, East Fairmount Park*). This lovely, brick Georgian mansion was erected in the 1760s on a laurel-covered hill overlooking the Schuylkill. (Check for tour availability at 215-235-1776 or go to www.laurelhillmansion.org. Admission is $8 for adults, $5 for seniors over 65, students and youths 13 to 17 and free for children 12 and under.)

Francis and Rebecca Rawle built the middle section of the house in 1760. Rebecca Rawle married Samuel Shoemaker in 1767 and added a kitchen wing. Laurel Hill was confiscated by the state legislature during the Revolution because of Shoemaker's pro-British sympathies and was sold to Maj. James Parr. The octagonal wing on the north side of the house was added after the Revolution. When wartime passions subsided, Rebecca Rawle Shoemaker bought Laurel Hill back and returned here in 1784. Dr. Phillip Syng Physick, father of American surgery, later purchased the house and in 1828 gave it to his daughter, Sally Randolph (hence the name Randolph Drive).

8 Leaving Laurel Hill, follow Randolph Drive north and east until it crosses Reservoir Drive and becomes Dauphin Drive. Pass the **Medicine Man** sculpture to **Woodford Mansion (8)** (*near 33rd and Dauphin Streets*), a Georgian house built in 1756. (Open 10 a.m. to 4 p.m. Wednesday through Sunday. Admission is $8 for adults; $5 for seniors 65 and over, students and youths 13 to 17; and free for children 12 and under. For more information, call 215-229-6115.)

Woodford was erected by William Coleman as a grouping of three buildings: a handsome brick house, and a separate servants' house and stable. Coleman, a friend of Benjamin Franklin, was a Philadelphia merchant and served as judge of the Supreme Court of Pennsylvania before his death in 1769. The mansion was subsequently owned by loyal British subjects, including David Franks and his daughter, Rebecca, who entertained Lord Howe, commander of the occupying British forces, here in the winter of 1777–78. In 1780, with the British troops gone, the Frankses were exiled and the house was in the hands of Quakers.

9 Make a left turn from Dauphin onto Greenland Drive, which becomes Strawberry Mansion Drive. Pass the front of Woodford on the way to nearby **Strawberry Mansion (9)** (*2450 Strawberry Mansion Drive near 33rd and Dauphin Streets*). This is the largest mansion in the park, featuring a Federal-style center section and Greek Revival wings. (Open 10 a.m. to 4 p.m. Wednesday through Sunday, March through December; 10 a.m. to 4 p.m. Saturdays in February; and by appointment in January. Admission is $8 for adults; $5 for seniors, students and youths 13 to 17; and free for children under 12.)

Strawberry Mansion got its name in the mid-19th century, when it was a dairy farm, serving strawberries and cream. The surrounding community has taken on the name. But long before that, the mansion was known as the home of Philadelphia judges. Quaker Judge William Lewis bought the wooded land in 1783 and rebuilt an earlier structure by about 1790, calling it "Summerville." Another judge, Joseph Hemphill, purchased the house in the 1820s and added the Greek Revival wings. Here, he entertained such guests as the Marquis de Lafayette, John C. Calhoun of South Carolina and Daniel Webster of Massachusetts. Hemphill's son, Coleman, grew strawberries here from roots he imported from Chile. The house has elegant Federal, Regency and Empire furniture.

10 Leaving Strawberry Mansion, make your way to nearby Ridge Avenue and follow it to **Laurel Hill Cemetery (10)** (*3822 Ridge Avenue*). This was the first cemetery in the nation designed by an architect and was a popular picnic spot during the 19th century. (Cemetery gates open daily 7 a.m. to 7 p.m., May 1 to October 31, and 7 a.m. to 5 p.m. from November 1 to April 30. Office, museum and gift shop open 8:30 a.m. to 4:30 p.m. Monday through Friday; 9:30 a.m. to 4:30 p.m. Saturday and Sunday. Free. Donations appreciated. Tours provided by appointment; call 215-228-8200.)

This sprawling Victorian necropolis was founded by John Jay Smith in 1836. The burial of the dead in churchyards led to crowding and health concerns and sparked an interest in developing a rural cemetery. Smith, the head of the Library Company of Philadelphia, acquired land on the banks of the Schuylkill and invited architects to submit designs.

John Notman, a young, Scottish-born architect, received the commission, beating out well-known architect William Strickland, de-

Laurel Hill Cemetery

Laurel Hill Cemetery

signer of the Second Bank of the United States. Notman laid out curving paths and sculpted natural amphitheaters out of the riverside slope, turning the park-like Laurel Hill into such a popular destination that tickets had to be handed out to control the number of visitors.

More than 70,000 people lie buried here in a beautiful, 100-acre sculpture garden, amid obelisks and mausoleums that dot the hilly landscape overlooking the river. Dozens of military commanders were interred in Laurel Hill—a kind of Valhalla of the Civil War, shared by enlisted men as well.

You can pick up a map at the gatehouse, located at the entrance to the cemetery. Walk down a narrow lane, through a canyon of brooding marble statues and granite monuments; pass a macabre tomb depicting a soul's escape from a sarcophagus; then look for a large, ivy-covered maple and a simple, white headstone beneath it. Here lies George Gordon Meade, the general who led Federal troops to victory at the Battle of Gettysburg.

Down another winding road is the tomb of Adm. John Adolph Bernard Dahlgren, "father of modern naval ordnance," who helped revolutionize the navies of the world and who developed the Dahlgren cannon. Next to him is his son, Col. Ulric Dahlgren, who was killed in 1864 during a cavalry raid near Richmond. And farther on is the grave of Confederate general John C. Pemberton, a Philadelphia native who surrendered Vicksburg, Mississippi, to Gen. Ulysses S. Grant with 30,000 Southern troops on Independence Day, 1863.

The rolling hills, with their forest of stone markers in all shapes and sizes, have many stories to tell. Take, for instance, the grave of Lt. Benjamin H. Hodgson. He died with the 7th Calvary at the Battle of the Little Bighorn in 1876. His final resting place is marked by a broken column, indicating the death of a young person whose life was cut short.

Another interesting historical note: Three men and three women who were first-class passengers on the ocean liner *Titanic* have markers here. The women survived the sinking in 1912. The men did not. Only one of the bodies, that of William Crothers Dulles, was recovered to be buried here. The other dead included George Dunton Widener and his son, Harry Elkins Widener. Their bodies were not recovered, but they have marker plaques. As a memorial to the two men, their family endowed the Widener Library at Harvard University.

Also buried here is Sarah Josepha Hale, editor of the magazine *Godey's Lady's Book* and author of the nursery rhyme best known as "Mary Had a Little Lamb."

11 Leave the cemetery and make a left turn at Ridge Avenue. Continue to Calumet Street, make a left, and follow it across the Falls Bridge. Turn left onto Martin Luther King Jr. Drive and take it to Montgomery Drive, make a right turn and follow Montgomery to Belmont Avenue. On your left is the **Ohio House (11)** (*Belmont Avenue near States Drive*), built for the Centennial Exhibition in 1876. This Victorian Gothic cottage represented the state of Ohio during the Centennial. It was erected with stone from 21 quarries in the state.

12 Head north on Belmont Avenue to Belmont Mansion Drive, then make a right turn for **Belmont Plateau** and **Belmont Mansion (12)** (*Belmont Mansion Drive, West Fairmount Park*). From the mansion grounds, you'll get a spectacular view of the city skyline. (Belmont Mansion is open 11 a.m. to 5 p.m. Tuesday through Friday and on weekends by appointment. Admission is $7 for adults; $5 for seniors 64 and over, students and children 6 to 18; and free to children under 6. For more information, call 215-878-8844.)

Ohio House

Belmont Plateau is more than 240 feet above the river, so it offers one of the best vistas of Philadelphia, looking down toward the art museum and the skyscrapers beyond. The Belmont Mansion belonged to Judge William Peters in 1742. Peters, a Loyalist, returned to England but his son Richard, a patriot, entertained Washington, Franklin and Madison here. Today, it's a favorite place for wedding receptions and private parties. Since 2007 the mansion has also hosted an **Underground Railroad Museum.**

⑬ Follow Belmont Mansion Drive until it forks, bear left, cross Montgomery Drive and bear left again for North Horticulture Drive and the **Horticulture Center (13)** (*North Horticultural Drive near Belmont Avenue, West Fairmount Park*). This is Philadelphia's only multipurpose horticultural exhibition facility. (Open 9 a.m. to 3 p.m. Monday and Tuesday; 9 a.m. to 10 p.m. Wednesday through Friday; 10 a.m. to 10 p.m. Saturday and 10 a.m. to 7 p.m. Sunday.) The center has permanent and changing seasonal plantings, a display room, greenhouse and meeting room. Its Christmas displays are a highlight of the season.

Shofuso
Japanese
House and
Garden

14 Follow Horticultural Drive to the **Shofuso Japanese House and Garden (14)** (*Lansdowne Drive near Belmont Avenue and Horticultural Drive, West Fairmount Park*), a reconstruction of a 17th-century Japanese scholar's house, tea house and garden. (Open 10 a.m. to 4 p.m. Wednesday through Friday, and 10 a.m. to 5 p.m. Saturday and Sunday from March through October. Open 10 a.m. to 4 p.m. Saturday and Sunday from November through December 15. Admission $12 for adults; $8 for seniors, children 5 to 17 and students with college ID; free for children under 5 and active-duty military with ID.)

The house was first exhibited at the Museum of Modern Art in New York, then reassembled here in the 1950s. It was refurbished by the Japanese government in 1976 as a gift in honor of the Bicentennial. It is called Shofuso, or "pine breeze villa," and has a serene feel to it.

Memorial Hall

15 Continue on Lansdowne Drive, make a left turn onto Belmont Avenue, then another left at Avenue of the Republic (formerly North Concourse Drive). Coming up on your left is **Memorial Hall (15)** (*Avenue of the Republic near 42nd Street and Parkside Avenue, West Fairmount Park*), the only major building remaining from the Centennial Exhibition of 1876. This magnificent building is home to the **Please Touch Museum (15)**, a children's museum as well as an events venue for elaborate weddings, bar and bat mitzvahs and corporate galas.

The museum is open 9 a.m. to 5 p.m. Monday and Tuesday, 10 a.m. to 5 p.m. on Wednesday, 9 a.m. to 5 p.m. Thursday through Saturday, and 11 a.m. to 5 p.m. on Sunday. Admission is $19.95 for adults and children age 1 and over. Children under 1 are free.

The state of Pennsylvania and City of Philadelphia built Memorial Hall between 1874 and 1876 at a cost of $1.5 million. An example of Beaux Arts architecture, it was designed by Hermann J. Schwarzmann to be an international art gallery and a permanent memorial to the centennial year of American independence. The massive green dome of the grand stone building can be seen above the trees from miles away by motorists on the Schuylkill Expressway.

After the exposition, the newly organized Pennsylvania Museum used the building. Memorial Hall housed art collections until 1954, when it was closed as a museum and turned over to the Fairmount Park Commission. For the next four years, the venerable building was vacant. It was later renovated and used for park offices and public functions and parties. The Great Hall, with its inlaid marble, translucent dome and creamy Victorian stucco work, became a popular site. Other parts of the building housed a swimming pool and gymnasium.

Today, the facility houses the popular Please Touch Museum, which teaches children the thrill of learning through play, interactive exhibits and special events. Memorial Hall is also known for an intricate, 20-by-40-foot model of the Centennial grounds and a fully restored and operating 1908 Dentzel Carousel with beautiful handcrafted animals. (Nearby—just north of the building—is an equestrian bronze of Gen. George Gordon Meade, victorious commander of Union forces at the Battle of Gettysburg in 1863.)

16 Continue on Avenue of the Republic to the **Smith Civil War Memorial (16)** (*Avenue of the Republic, West Fairmount Park*), a monument built from 1897 to 1912 to honor Pennsylvania's heroes in the war.

The memorial was designed by James H. and John T. Windrim and built under a bequest of Richard Smith at a cost of about $500,000. The two equestrian bronze statues represent Gen. Winfield S. Hancock and Gen. George B. McClellan. Other statues immortalize Gen. George Gordon Meade and Gen. John F. Reynolds. Busts of Pennsylvania governor Andrew G. Curtin and other Army and Navy heroes are part of the memorial, which is divided into two parts with towers rising overhead.

17 Turn left after leaving the memorial and follow Lansdowne Drive to Sweetbriar Lane. Make a right there and a left on Cedar Grove Drive heading to **Cedar Grove (17)** (*1 Cedar Grove Drive, West Fairmount Park*), a gray fieldstone house erected about 1748 in the Frankford section of Philadelphia. It was dismantled and moved here in 1926. (Open for guided public tours at 11 a.m., 1 p.m. and 2:30 p.m. Thursday through Sunday from April through December; first Sunday of each month, tours from 10 a.m. to 4 p.m. Tours by appointment from January through March. Admission $8 for adults;

$5 for seniors over 65, students and youths 13 to 17; children 12 and under free.)

Elizabeth Coates Paschall, a widow, built the house on land in Frankford adjacent to her father's farm. Elizabeth's granddaughter, Sarah Paschall Morris, inherited the house and added on to it in the 1790s. The piazza was built in the 1840s. Lydia Thompson Morris, fifth-generation owner of Cedar Grove, had the house disassembled, then erected in Fairmount Park as a gift to the city. Inside is the furniture of five generations, reflecting the changing styles, including William and Mary, Queen Anne, Chippendale and Federal.

⓲ Head back toward the Smith Memorial, then bear left on Sweetbriar Lane for **Sweetbriar (18)** (*1 Sweetbriar Lane, near Lansdowne Drive, West Fairmount Park*), a symmetrical, Federal-style mansion built in 1797. (Closed while undergoing renovations.)

Sweetbriar

The house was built by Samuel and Jean Breck to escape the yellow fever epidemics that killed thousands of Philadelphians between 1793 and 1800. The Brecks entertained such influential people as the Marquis de Lafayette when he toured the United States in 1825.

⑲ Our next stop is another historic house transplanted from its original setting. Returning to the traffic circle near the Smith Memorial, follow Lansdowne Drive south and east to the **Letitia Street House (19)** (*West Girard Avenue and 34th Street, West Fairmount Park*), a brick house built in the early 1700s on Letitia Street, between Front and Second Streets, and moved here in 1883. The site was rehabilitated and restored in recent years and has housed a community development corporation, which works to preserve, promote and revitalize neighborhoods.

⑳ Across the street from the Letitia Street House is the **Philadelphia Zoo (20)** (*West Girard Avenue and 34th Street, West Fairmount Park*), America's first zoological park and home to more than 2,000 animals from around the world. (Open 9:30 a.m. to 4 p.m. daily from January 1 through February, and 9:30 a.m. to 5 p.m. daily from March 1 through October. Closed Thanksgiving, Christmas Eve, Christmas Day, New Year's Eve and New Year's Day. Admission $24

Philadelphia Zoo's Siberian tigers

Philadelphia Zoo's swan boats

for adults 12 and above; $19 ages 2 to 11; and free for children under 2. Winter admission through March 15 is $16 for adults and children. Parking is $16.)

When the zoo opened in 1874, nobody had seen anything like it—at least not in America. Beyond the ornate iron gates in West Fairmount Park were wonders found only in the pages of travel books. Thousands waited to get in—men in bowler hats, women in long, full dresses. More arrived every minute, in horse-drawn carriages, streetcars and steamboats chugging up the Schuylkill.

At 9 o'clock on a warm, clear morning, while a brass band played and flags rustled in the breeze, America's first zoo opened. Admission was 25 cents, 10 cents for children. And it was worth every penny. Inside were an Indian elephant and a Tasmanian devil, Australian wombats and dingoes, wallabies and kangaroos. There were bears from Brigham Young's collection in Salt Lake City and a prairie dog village, an attraction found nowhere else in an urban setting.

For our tour, collect your ticket at one of the Victorian gatehouses designed by architect Frank Furness and erected in 1876. Pass through the iron gates and enter a world that mixes old and new. More than 500 species inhabit the zoo, compared to 43 when the attraction opened. Six species of marsupials, or pouched animals, are housed here—about half the number the early zoo had. Other animals that once lived here have become extinct over the past century, such as the West Indian monk seal, the toolache wallaby, the passenger pigeon and the Carolina parakeet. But the new zoo has had many residents that the old zoo didn't have, including naked mole rats and white lions.

One of the sights that greeted the first visitors was startling. On opening day, Jennie, an Indian elephant, appeared to be wandering through the zoo without any restraints. The high grass around her obscured a chain holding her in place near the Bear Pits. Several people, seeing an elephant moving toward them, fled for their lives, according to old newspaper accounts.

Other attractions common to zoos today were absent: lions, tigers, zebras and camels. That was remedied in the first few months. Six giraffes arrived on August 11, 1874, and a pair of lions, a Bengal tiger and a black leopard made their debut on December 28 of that year. The first African elephant came on New Year's Eve. The zoo became a big hit. Throngs of people came out to see the strange animals from across the world. Women shaded themselves from the sun with parasols. Children rode in small wagons pulled by goats.

Today, there are no goat rides. But you can pedal a swan boat on a lake, zip through the air on the WildWorks Rope course, hop on a colorful hand-painted carousel or ride a train through the zoo.

Begin strolling the path along 34th Street, following it past the kangaroos at the Outback Outpost, then head over to the new Penguin Point exhibit and Bear Country, one of the most enduring attractions. While spectators watch them, free-roaming peacocks step across the walkway, as if they were visitors. Heading south along 34th Street, you pass between the African Plains exhibits, stocked with antelope, zebra, giraffes and wart hogs.

Further on are Red Panda Pass, Otter Falls and Raptor Ridge, and as you loop back, the Bird House and the popular Primate Reserve, where gorillas, gibbons, ruffed and blue-eyed lemurs, langurs, colobus monkeys, squirrel monkeys and orangutans roam. Nearby are Big Cat Falls and the Reptile and Amphibian House.

The oldest building in the zoo is Solitude, the manor house of John Penn, grandson of William Penn. Most of the zoo's original buildings have been replaced since World War II, but several historic structures, such as this one, remain. The neoclassical house was built between 1784 and 1785.

The zoo is ever changing. If planners have their way, the facility will always be part zoo, part garden and part theme park.

Germantown and Chestnut Hill

Germantown and Chestnut Hill

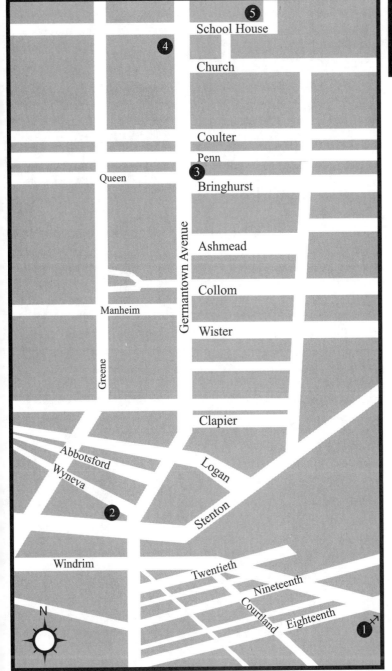

School House

Church

Coulter

Penn

Queen

Bringhurst

Germantown Avenue

Ashmead

Collom

Manheim

Wister

Greene

Clapier

Abbotsford

Logan

Wyneva

Stenton

Windrim

Twentieth

Nineteenth

Courtland

Eighteenth

N

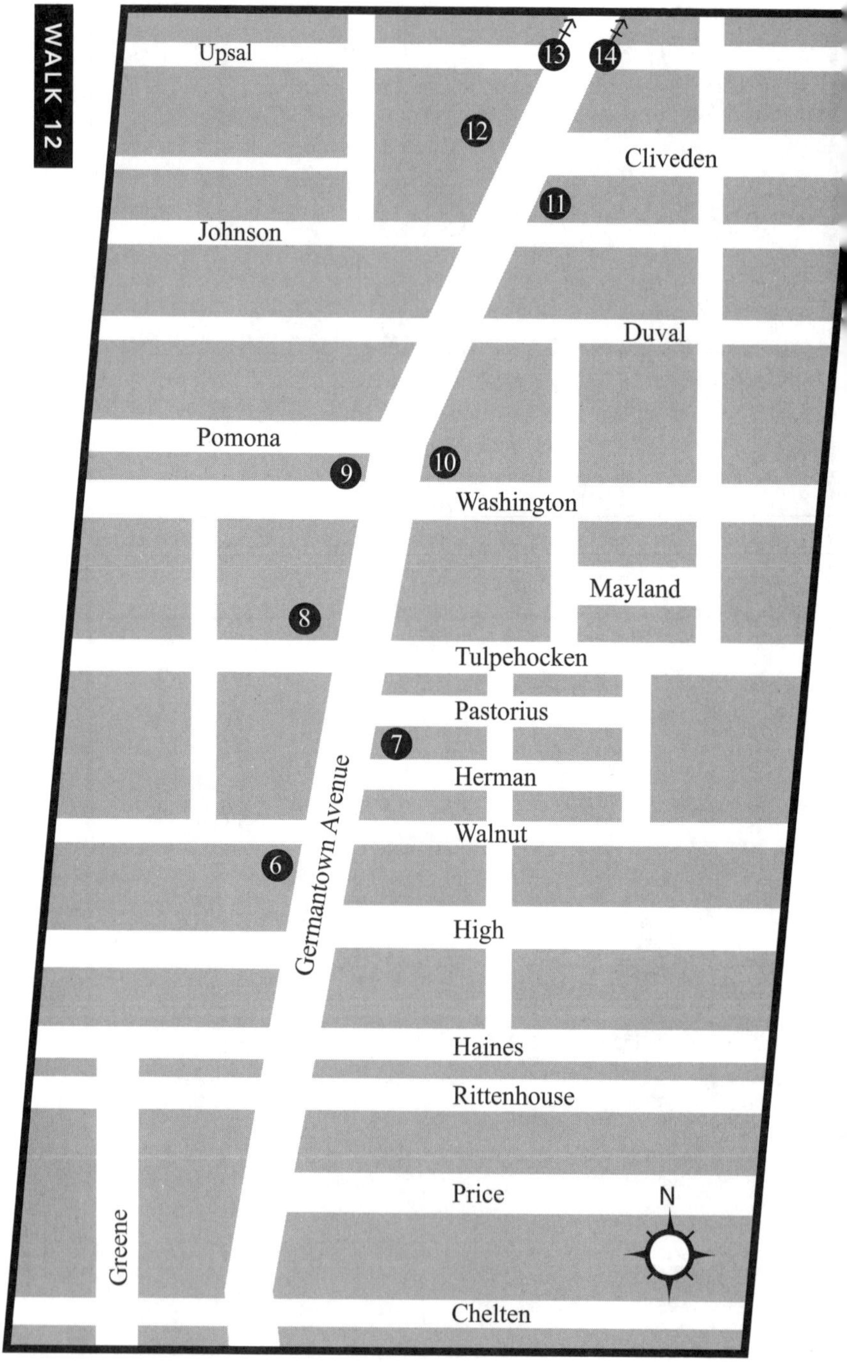

Upsal

⑬ ⑭

⑫

Cliveden

⑪

Johnson

Duval

Pomona

⑨ ⑩

Washington

Mayland

⑧

Tulpehocken

Pastorius

⑦

Herman

Walnut

⑥

High

Haines

Rittenhouse

Germantown Avenue

Price

N

Greene

Chelten

USEFUL INFORMATION

Germantown, Mount Airy and Chestnut Hill provide a variety of restaurants. Among them are CinCin, which offers Chinese cuisine popular with Chestnut Hill residents, at 7838 Germantown Avenue, and Jansen, in a beautiful historic house at 7402 Germantown Avenue. Also Trattoria Moma for Italian cuisine at 7131 Germantown Avenue; and Chestnut Grill and Sidewalk Cafe at 8229 Germantown Avenue.

For ambience and a sense of history, don't miss the Valley Green Inn, built in 1850. In nice weather, on a Sunday, you can eat brunch on the porch and watch kids feeding the ducks in the Wissahickon, not to mention all the joggers and bikers and horse riders passing by on Forbidden Drive. The inn is located on Valley Green Road at Wissahickon Creek.

For these tours, parking is available on the streets, often at meters, sometimes at lots set aside at the historic sites. Though driving is probably the best course, you also can reach Germantown by taking SEPTA's Route 23 bus. Board it at 11th and Market Streets in Center City and get off in Germantown at Queen Lane. This location puts you close to several sites that are within walking distance.

Introduction

Germantown took its name from early settlers: German and Dutch Quakers and Mennonites who were seeking religious freedom. The new arrivals came to Philadelphia in 1683 and moved onto a large tract of land purchased by the Frankfurt Land Company from William Penn. The company's German agent, Francis Daniel Pastorius, helped the group and soon became the most influential member of the community. A single-street village was laid out. And over the next few years, a Quaker meetinghouse was constructed of logs, and homes and orchards stretched along the road for about a mile.

Germantown's industry also developed and, with it, the population increased. The first grist mill in the Philadelphia area was built here in 1683, and America's first paper mill was erected here in 1690.

The community received a borough charter in 1691, allowing the residents to have their own mayor, council, court and market. The area became a township in 1707 and remained so until it was absorbed by the City of Philadelphia in 1854.

Germantown has had a tradition of progressive thinking. Just as settlers originally were drawn here for the religious freedom guaranteed by Penn, so, too, were they strongly supportive of other individual liberties, sometimes ahead of their time. The first written protest against Negro slavery was penned in Germantown in 1688 and sent by Pastorius and other Mennonites to a Friends Meeting. A street in Germantown today bears Pastorius' name. The community also found itself in the forefront of the fight for freedom and independence in 1777, when forces under George Washington attacked the British in the Battle of Germantown during the Revolutionary War.

After the war, Germantown became a place to which wealthy Philadelphia residents resorted for relief from the summer heat. It was a half-day's carriage ride from Philadelphia, about six miles away, and its higher elevation and rural surroundings offered slightly cooler temperatures. Some city residents established country homes here, several of which are part of our walking and riding tour.

Much of this tour is best done by car, though you will often find clusters of historic sites that can be made into mini-walks. If you continue driving northwest on Germantown Avenue, you will pass through Mount Airy on your way to Chestnut Hill, a charming village of specialty shops, galleries, antique stores and restaurants.

Chestnut Hill looks more like the suburbs than the city. It started as a colonial settlement of farmhouses and taverns and grew over the years, spurred by the establishment of a rail line in 1884 that brought vacationers from Philadelphia. Many of those visitors liked the area so much they decided to stay, building Queen Anne and Colonial Revival–style houses. The Germantown Road was the main route to Reading, Bethlehem and other northwest communities, and the stretch of it from Wayne Junction to the city limits at Chestnut Hill College has been placed on the National Register of Historic Places.

The Tour

❶ For our first stop, head northwest on Germantown Avenue to the 4400 block, make a right turn on Windrim Avenue and follow it four blocks to **Stenton (1)** (*4601 18th Street at Windrim Avenue*),

Stenton

a house designed by William Penn's secretary, James Logan, and finished in 1730. (Open 1 to 4 p.m. Tuesday through Saturday, April 1 through December 22; open other times by appointment. Closed December 23 to January 1. Open by appointment January 2 to March 31. Admission $8 for adults; $6 for students, children and seniors; children under 6 free. For more information, call 215-329-7312.)

For half a century, after Penn returned to England in 1701, Logan represented the interests of the Penn family here. As such, he was one of the city's most influential leaders. (Logan Circle is named for him.) The son of a Scottish Quaker schoolmaster, he was a businessman, farmer and intellectual who excelled in linguistics, mathematics and other scholarly pursuits. He named Stenton after the birthplace of his father. Though the grounds are now surrounded by urban sprawl, the house was among the first country manors outside Philadelphia and was the first Queen Anne–style building constructed in the area. It is encircled by hemlocks, gardens and outbuildings that were part of the original plantation of more than 500 acres.

Gen. Sir William Howe, commander of the occupying British forces in Philadelphia during the Revolutionary War, used the house while he was plotting his moves during the Battle of Germantown in 1777. George Washington also occupied Stenton briefly earlier that year on his way south to try to stop the British at the Battle of Brandywine.

The entrance hall is large, the staircase wide and the dining room and library also expansive. Logan accumulated 2,500 books for his library, one of the largest in the colonies, with the major collection of volumes on linguistics, the sciences and the classics. The Logan library was bequeathed to the Library Company of Philadelphia.

❷ Return to your car and continue northwest on Germantown Avenue to **Loudoun (2)** (*4650 Germantown Avenue at East Abbottsford Avenue*), a graceful, Federal-style house built about 1801

Loudoun

Grumblethorpe

and given a Greek Revival look by 1830. The house and grounds are well maintained and are worth seeing, but interior tours were discontinued after the house and furniture were damaged by fire. (Not open to the public.)

Loudoun's owner, Thomas Armat, named the house after Loudoun County, Virginia, the first place he settled after coming to America from England. The Greek Revival portico was constructed in 1830, and a wing was added later. Loudoun remained in the Armat family for many years until it was deeded to the Fairmount Park Commission in 1939.

❸ About six blocks up Germantown Avenue you will come to **Grumblethorpe (3)** (*5267 Germantown Avenue*), a charming, rustic stone house built in 1744 by Philadelphia wine importer and merchant John Wister. (For information on tours, call 215-843-4820 or 215-844-1683. Admission $8; students and seniors $6; family $20; and groups of 10 or more $5 per person.)

An architectural treasure, this German farmstead was constructed from stone quarried on the property and the joists were carved from nearby oaks. The house has lower ceilings and a more rustic feel than the other houses on the tour. It was originally built as a summer home but later became Wister's year-round residence. During the American Revolution, Grumblethorpe served as head-quarters for British general James Agnew. The house remained in the Wister family for 160 years. Visitors will find a warm simplicity to the rooms and handsome period furniture.

④ Continue north two blocks to the **Deshler-Morris House (4)** (*5442 Germantown Avenue*), the official residence of President George Washington during two separate stays that each lasted a few weeks in 1793 and 1794. (Currently closed except for special events. When the site reopens, the National Park Service expects to have hours on Saturdays from Memorial Day to Labor Day. Admission free. For more information, call 215-965-2305.)

This stone house was built in 1772 by David Deshler, a prominent Quaker merchant in Philadelphia. The house was in the middle of fighting between Continental and British troops during the Battle of

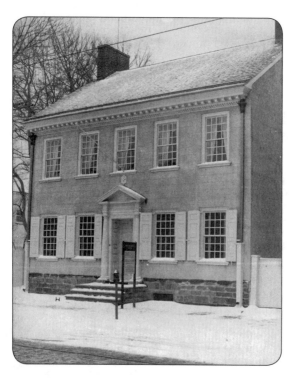

Deshler-Morris House

Germantown on October 4, 1777, and was subsequently occupied by Howe, the commander of British forces.

The next owner, Isaac Franks, leased the house to President Washington in 1793 during the yellow fever epidemic in Philadelphia, the young nation's capital. Washington presided here over four meetings of his divided cabinet, which included Thomas Jefferson, Alexander Hamilton, Henry Knox and Edmund Randolph. Heated debate broke out during the meetings on what position the country should take in the war between England and France. The president and his family returned to the house during July 1794.

They sometimes crossed historic **Market Square**—just across Germantown Avenue from the house—to worship at a German Reformed church. The church, erected in 1733, no longer stands but the square remains, a remnant of the days when much of the community's activity took place out of doors: stalls with vendors' goods were here, and miscreants were locked up in public stocks. Today, the square is presided over by a statue of a Union soldier, which has been standing there at solitary rest since 1883. The statue is mounted atop a slab of granite from Devil's Den, one of the hot spots of fighting during the Battle of Gettysburg in 1863.

The Germantown "White House" was sold by Franks to Elliston and John Perot and later was owned by Elliston's son-in-law, Samuel B. Morris, in the 1830s. Its architectural design is handsome, with a pediment over the front door, shutters and dentil work over the second-floor windows. Inside is elegant period furniture. Don't miss the splendid gardens on the side and back of the house.

❺ Cross Germantown Avenue and walk through Market Square to the **Germantown Historical Society (5)** (*5501 Germantown Avenue*), located in a Colonial Revival building that contains a visitors center, a museum and a library that gives a history of Germantown and information on many local historic sites. (Open 9 a.m. to 1 p.m. Tuesday, 1 to 5 p.m. Thursday and by appointment on Sunday. Library and archives admission $10; students, $5. Museum admission $3; seniors and students, $2. For more information, call 215-844-1683.)

The historical society, located in a spacious building that once served as a bank, offers a good introduction to the area. Visit the library for more detailed study and see antique furniture, china and quilts in the museum. You can pick up maps and free brochures here about the places we'll be visiting.

Wyck

6 Now drive about half a mile up Germantown Avenue to **Wyck (6)** (*6026 Germantown Avenue*), one of the oldest houses in Philadelphia, erected in 1690 by Hans Milan. (Open 12 to 4 p.m. Thursday through Saturday, April through November. Tours December through March by appointment. Donations encouraged. For information, call 215-848-1690.)

Wyck is not really one house, but two. Milan built the first Quaker-style house, then another alongside for his daughter and her husband. The two houses were joined—and were used by nine generations of the same family. This large home contains three centuries of simple, original furniture befitting its Quaker occupants. It also features a large, early-19th-century garden.

The original log structure from 1690 was replaced sometime between 1710 and 1715 with a stone house. It received a stucco finish in 1799, then got a Greek Revival makeover in 1824. The house had more work done on it in 1999, including a new slate roof. Wyck was used as a British field hospital during the Battle of Germantown in 1777 and was visited by the Marquis de Lafayette on his return tour of America in 1825.

7 Next up is the **Mennonite Meetinghouse (7)** (*6121 Germantown Avenue*), erected in 1770 by members of the Mennonite religious sect, who were among the founders of Germantown in 1683. The building is located next to the **Germantown Mennonite Historic Trust** (*6133 Germantown Avenue*), which provides information on the meeting house. (Suggested donation for meetinghouse tour is $5 per adult. Call 215-843-0943 to schedule a tour or receive more information.) Here, exhibits tell the story of the Mennonites' arrival in the area. On display are a variety of Bibles and Psalm books printed in German in Germantown during the colonial period. One of the most prized artifacts is a desk from which the first known protest against slavery in America was written in 1688.

❽ Drive another block up Germantown Avenue to Tulpehocken Street and make a left turn for the **Ebenezer Maxwell Mansion (8)** (*200 West Tulpehocken Street*), the beautiful, mid-19th-century stone villa of a prosperous businessman—and now an authentically restored Victorian house museum. (Open for tours at12:15, 1:15, 2:15 and 3:15 p.m. Thursday, Friday and Saturday and other times

Ebenezer
Maxwell
Mansion

by appointment. It is closed from early December through February. Admission $8 for adults, $6 for students and youths 18 and under. For more information, call 215-438-1861.)

Ebenezer Maxwell owned a large department store in Philadelphia, shipping goods out to customers before the practice became widely used. He was among the first of the wealthy businessmen to live outside of the downtown area and commute to work by train.

The house, built in 1859, is pure Victorian, from the high ceilings to the extravagant wallpapers. It exhibits Philadelphia-made period furniture and household goods.

9 Get back on Germantown Avenue and continue a block and a half northwest to the **Johnson House (9)** (*6306 Germantown Avenue*), an 18th-century house that became a stop on the Underground Railroad for escaped slaves during the 19th century. (Open for walk-in tours at 1:15, 2:15 and 3:15 p.m. Saturday throughout the year; open 10 a.m. to 4 p.m. Thursday and Friday from early February to early June and from early September to late November. Other tours on Monday, Tuesday and Wednesday by appointment with two weeks' notice. Admission $10 for adults; $7 for seniors over 55; and $4 for children 12 and under. For more information, call 215-438-1768.)

This fine example of Germantown architecture was built for John Johnson in 1768 and was home to three generations of a Quaker family that worked to abolish slavery and improve living conditions for African Americans. As a station on the Underground Railroad in the 1850s, the house provided shelter for blacks as they made their way to freedom.

10 Now cross Germantown Avenue and stop at the **Concord School House (10)** (*6309 Germantown Avenue*), a one-room school built in 1775. (Open for guided and self-guided tours. Admission free. Donation of $5 is suggested for adults and $3 for students and children. For information on tours and hours, call 215-844-1683.)

This two-and-a-half-story building, with a simple belfry, was constructed by local craftsmen, and the first classes were held in October 1775. Inside are a small fireplace and hard wooden benches used by children of those early days. The school house still has its original bell, as well as the original schoolmaster's desk.

Adjacent to the school is the **Upper Burying Ground**, the oldest burial ground in Germantown, dating to 1692. Among those interred here are soldiers from the Battle of Germantown, the War of 1812 and the Civil War.

① A short distance farther on Germantown Avenue is one of the most magnificent and historic colonial houses in Philadelphia, **Cliveden (11)** (*6401 Germantown Avenue*). It was the elegant country seat of Pennsylvania Chief Justice Benjamin Chew in colonial days and the scene of a major clash in the Battle of Germantown on October 4, 1777. (Open noon to 4 p.m. Thursday through Sunday from May through August, and noon to 4 p.m. Friday through Sunday from September to late November. Tours begin on the hour. Appointments can be made to tour the site December through April. Admission $10 for adults and seniors; $8 for students and AAA members; free for children 6 years and under. For more information, call 215-848-1777.)

The Georgian stone house, built between 1763 and 1767, has a wonderful balance and symmetry, with a pediment over the doorway that is repeated at the roof. It now sits on a six-acre piece of ground, though Chew owned 60 acres.

Cliveden

This peaceful, tree-shaded property was transformed into a war zone in 1777. The British occupying forces were expecting to spend a quiet fall in Germantown when Gen. George Washington ordered a surprise attack before dawn on the foggy morning of October 4. British advance units were forced to retreat before a hail of gunfire and superior numbers.

But 100 to 120 Redcoats stubbornly held on at Cliveden, taking cover behind its two-foot-thick walls. They withstood a cannon bombardment and several charges before the Americans were forced to fall back across a wider front because of British reinforcements and American confusion over troop deployments. The bulk of the fighting had taken place in the center of Germantown behind fences and around buildings.

Today, visitors can still see outside walls scarred by bullets. Recreations of the battle have been held at the site as part of the Revolutionary Germantown Festival activities in October. The roar of the cannon and rattle of musketry have been heard here again as "Redcoats" seek refuge in the gray stone house.

Cliveden is filled with splendid furniture from the 18th century, and the estate includes outbuildings and a barn that serves as a gift shop. Descendants of Benjamin Chew lived at the house until 1972. It is now a property of the National Trust for Historic Preservation.

12 As you leave Cliveden, cross Germantown Avenue for another landmark, **Upsala (12)** (*6430 Germantown Avenue*), a Federal-style house that is believed to have been built in the mid-18th century. It was used by American troops during the Battle of Germantown. (The house was purchased in 2017 and is privately owned. The property can be rented for weddings and film and TV productions.)

The name comes from the university city of Uppsala in Sweden. The house was owned by the Johnsons, a family of tanners, and remained in the hands of their descendants into the 20th century. American troops set up artillery on the property to shell the British at Cliveden.

If you're ready for a break, stop at a restaurant in **Chestnut Hill**, which stretches from the 7900 block to the 8700 block of Germantown Avenue. The hilly streets and colonial decor give a strong village feel to this community. There are two more stops on our tour, and this is a good place to have lunch and read up on the area's history.

Upsala

13 When you're ready to resume the tour, continue on Germantown Avenue to the **Woodmere Art Museum (13)** (*9201 Germantown Avenue*), where paintings, sculpture, photographs and prints by American and European artists of the 19th and early 20th centuries are exhibited. (Open 10 a.m. to 5 p.m. Tuesday through Thursday, 10 a.m. to 8 p.m. Friday, 10 a.m. to 6 p.m. Saturday, and 10 a.m. to 5 p.m. Sunday. Admission $10 for adults, $7 for seniors and free for children and students. Sundays are free. For information, call 215-247-0476.)

The museum was established in 1940 and is located in the Victorian mansion of its founder, Charles Knox Smith, who died in 1916. The five-story, 19th-century house, with handsome mansard roofs, has gallery space, a library and offices. The collection—including paintings by Mary Cassatt and Benjamin West—is dedicated to the art and artists of Philadelphia.

14 Return to Germantown Avenue and drive north to the 9500 block, where you will make a right turn on Hillcrest Avenue for the **Morris Arboretum of the University of Pennsylvania (14)** (*100*

East Northwestern Avenue; enter on Hillcrest Avenue between German-town and Stenton Avenues in Chestnut Hill). The arboretum contains more than 100 acres of gardens and landscaped property. (Open 10 a.m. to 4 p.m. daily, with extended hours in certain seasons. Admission $20 for adults; $18 for seniors 65 and over; $10 for students, youths 3 to 17 and active and retired military with ID; free for children under 3.)

Located on Philadelphia's border with Montgomery County, the arboretum was started in 1887 by John Morris and his sister, Lydia. She gave it to the university in 1932. Today, visitors enjoy a magnificent collection of mature trees, a swan pond, formal rose gardens and art such as *Two Lines*, a sculpture by George Rickey. Check out the garden railway featuring model trains and cable cars. Walk through a meadow, an English garden and a Japanese garden. The years seem to slip away as you stroll along paved winding pathways, through garden designs that take you back to the Victorian era.

Visitors to Philadelphia marvel that within the confines of a city founded more than 300 years ago, there are still quiet, elegant places like this. Changing demographics and old age have left many once-fashionable blocks of Germantown rundown and neglected, as you saw driving up Germantown Avenue. At the same time, efforts to save and restore the old stone houses of Mount Airy and Chestnut Hill and other properties have stabilized and reinvigorated those

Morris Arboretum of the University of Pennsylvania

Etruscan Love
Temple at
the Morris
Arboretum

neighborhoods.For residents and visitors alike, the treasures tucked away here, waiting to be discovered, will pay back the diligent walker of these neighborhoods with unending delight.

Philadelphia, a city that cherishes its past, shares it again with each new generation.

Photo Credits

WALK 1. P. 9, Philadelphia Inquirer. P. 10, Philadelphia Daily News. Pp. 11 & 15, Philadelphia Inquirer. P. 20, National Park Service—Thomas L. Davies. P. 22, American Philosophical Society. P. 23, Philadelphia Inquirer. P. 25, Inquirer Archives. Pp. 26, 27, 30, 32, Philadelphia Inquirer.

WALK 2. Pp. 41, 43, 46, 47, 48, Philadelphia Inquirer. P. 53, Inquirer Archives. P. 54, Philadelphia Daily News. Pp. 56 & 57, Philadelphia Inquirer.

WALK 3. Pp. 65, 69, 71, 73, 74, 76, 77, Philadelphia Inquirer. Pp. 78 & 79, Inquirer Archives.

WALK 4. Pp. 86, 88, 89, 90, 91, 92, 93, 95, Philadelphia Inquirer. P. 97, Philadelphia Daily News.

WALK 5. P. 105, Philadelphia Inquirer. P. 106, Inquirer Archives. P. 107, Philadelphia Inquirer. P. 108, Inquirer Archives. P. 109, Philadelphia Daily News. Pp. 110 & 111, Philadelphia Inquirer.

WALK 6. P. 118, Philadelphia Daily News. Pp. 119 & 120, Philadelphia Inquirer. P. 125, Inquirer Archives. P. 127, Philadelphia Inquirer. P. 129, Philadelphia Daily News. P. 130, Philadelphia Inquirer.

WALK 7. Pp. 136, 137, 138, 140, 143, 144, 147, Philadelphia Inquirer. P. 151, The Library Company of Philadelphia.

WALK 8. Pp. 158 & 159, Philadelphia Inquirer. P. 160, The Curtis Institute of Music/Jerome Lukowicz. P. 161, Inquirer Archives. P. 164, Philadelphia Inquirer.

WALK 9. P. 172, Inquirer Archives. Pp. 173 & 174, Philadelphia Inquirer. P. 175, Philadelphia Daily News. Pp. 177, 179, 180, 181, Philadelphia Inquirer.

WALK 10. Pp. 187 & 189, Philadelphia Inquirer. P. 190, Inquirer Archives. Pp. 192, 194, 195, 197, 199, 200, Philadelphia Inquirer.

WALK 11. Pp. 214 & 215, Philadelphia Inquirer. P. 217, Inquirer Archives. Pp. 218, 219, 221, 222, 223, Philadelphia Inquirer.

WALK 12. Pp. 231, 232, 233, 234, 236, 237, 239, Philadelphia Inquirer. P. 241, Philadelphia City Archives. Pp. 242 & 243, Philadelphia Inquirer.

Index